DR. JEFFERY CHAPMAN SR.

ACKNOWLEDGEMENTS

There are too many people who have influenced my life over the years to name here, but I would especially like to show gratitude to my family and friends. To the members of Raleigh North Christian Center, thank you for your constant support. And to everyone who played a role in helping this book come to life, thank you.

DEDICATION

This book wouldn't have been possible without the love and support of my best friend and wife of over 35 years. Thank you for seeing this book inside me and pushing me to get it written. I dedicate this to you, Sandie.

WHY I WROTE THIS BOOK?

Welcome to the, INCREASE: You Are Thinking Too Low, book. It is my prayer that you find it entertaining, informative, inspiring and very relatable. I am adamant about being as transparent as I can. Why? Because I do not want people to JUST read the highlight reel of my life. Not only is that deceiving but it also promotes a false, unattainable, "When I accept my calling to either ministry or the marketplace, everything will go smoothly, and everything I plan will work out the first time I try it," sort of reality. I almost hate to pop your bubble but EVERY ministry leader and entrepreneur you follow goes through trials, heartache and seasons of growth; it is inevitable and VERY necessary.

Yes, I will share the great things God has done in my life, ministry and family but I will also share the seasons of struggle and less than perfect circumstances. In the end, I am thankful for all of it because God used it ALL for my good. Initially, I wrote this book for God's people only. But then I saw the gross disconnect between the promises of God in the Bible, and how His people were living. Soon another layer revealed itself, as I spent more time speaking and interacting with clients, fellow business owners and acquaintances, the more I realized that low or limited mindset is not confined to the church only, but in fact, it is a malady that also affects people outside the church walls.

Therefore, this book will also benefit lay individuals that want to change the way they look at EVERYTHING that is or could be available to them.

It all starts with having the right mindset. But what if you don't know what that is? Don't worry. I will share how I developed that mindset and how you can as well. I am called to share this information with believers and the world. I want, and need, to break all the negative and erroneous religious traditions that have been holding people hostage for far too long. People need to change their mindset about what is available to them. For example, many don't believe all of God's financial blessings are available for them as well. Such fallacious beliefs have been promoted due to ignorance, jealousy, over-zealous leaders or just from fear of the unknown, and I believe they have been perpetuated long enough. It is time for God's people and the world to experience abundance without limits.

This message is NOT just for the people in church; it is for EVERYONE. What is the message? God's principles for wealth work; but unfortunately, God's people seem to be the only ones not leveraging them. Why do I say that? Because the world has for a very long time used the very same principles to build wealth, and guess what? It has worked for them. It is high time we embrace these principles and teach them to our children as well. Maybe you are reading this book and you are already acquainted with the Bible's wealth principles I will be sharing but you don't know their origin, why they were put in place and how to apply them properly. This book will help you answer those questions.

We live in America, the land of opportunity, but a large number of God's people don't see it this way, especially black churches. Why? Because many tend to have a, "The man is keeping me down," mentality. The funny thing is that, often, the man is way too busy making money to concoct plans to ruin/hold them back or keep them down.

This short-sided mindset also affects stability (or lack thereof) in families. How? Many change their living situation too often instead of taking the necessary steps to owning a home. They don't entertain the possibility of home ownership because they live paycheck-to-paycheck and don't know how to manage their finances properly. Others struggle with the notion that if a Christian leader is prospering (or living large), then they must be a "prosperity Gospel preacher." We have seen and experienced first-hand the pushback because we have a prospering church and an abundant life. Unfortunately, that is not the saddest part. The saddest part is that they cannot accept wealth for themselves either.

But why is having money seen as such a negative thing? And, since many pastors do not want that negative perception or cloud over them, they choose to remain in poverty and struggle when in reality, more is available for them. Let's talk about how the world outside the church sees wealth:

- Something to strive towards (or one might say, strive for)
- Wealth is good and taught openly and often
- Living well (balling) is a good thing
- Planning and saving for the future are a must
- Often reading and learning more about wealth is normal

Do you see the difference in how the world thinks and the inaccurate Christian mentality that promotes it is better to be poor than rich (many teachers often quote John 12:8 to back this teaching, but later in the book we will explore what Jesus actually meant by that statement). Many pastors/leaders struggle and promote thoughts that indicate struggling is the only way to live. Naturally that pushes their congregations towards the religious tradition of being humble or having a false sense of humility. Such thinking has people stuck in a vicious, and often, generational poverty cycle. Some are "so spiritual that they are no earthly good." You have heard that phrase before, right? What do I mean by that? Their kids and marriages are neglected because they are "too spiritual" or spend too much time only doing ministry work. We are called to be balanced people, and that includes taking care of our families as outlined in 1 Timothy 3:1-5 NASB,

It is a trustworthy statement: if any man aspires to the office of overseer, it is a fine work he desires to do. 2 An overseer, then, must be above reproach, the husband of one wife, temperate, prudent, respectable, hospitable, able to teach, 3 not addicted to wine or pugnacious, but gentle, peaceable, free from the love of money. 4 He must be one who manages his own household well, keeping his children under control with all dignity 5 (but if a man does not know how

to manage his own household, how will he take
care of the church of God?).

Why is this? Because many pastors are heavy on the spiritual aspect but neglect their earthly responsibilities. Why? Because they are too focused on "good things" to spend time with the people that REALLY matter. Yes, ministry is important but not at the cost of family, and in many instances, one's health. One must lead a balanced life and cultivate a mindset that says: "I am going to prosper. It's okay to own a thriving business." What goals do you have? Where do you want to be in five years? I cannot endorse enough having a 5-year family and ministry plan! (We will explore this concept further inside the, Increase Academy).

As you can see, I will be covering a wide range of areas and subjects in this book; areas you probably did not think had anything to do with wealth, but absolutely do. You might be wondering, "Why not just write a book about economics or financial principles then?" Because even though such books are great, they are not complete. Many of them are not complete because they do not include the Bible's principles about wealth. In order to fully appreciate God's comprehensive concept of wealth we must explore it from a holistic point of view.

What is wealth? Life more abundantly in ALL areas, including health/wellness, finances, mindset, body, soul and spirit. Living paycheck to paycheck may feel like the norm to you right now, but what is the opposite of that? The limited list below may have some items you may not be acquainted with, but you should be by the time you finish reading this book:

- Paying all the bills and having money left
- Managing money well
- Desire to buy/build a home(s)
- Taking care of your body/temple
- Investing in healthy food
- Joining a gym (wealth and health go together like a wink and a smile)
- Routinely speaking God's promises over your life (don't rehearse the problem, speak life and not death instead. A great habit to develop)

Be positive instead of negative. Thriving instead of sick and struggling. (Later in the book we will explore the thoughts necessary to replace this current low thinking mentality. Also, I have put together a robust list of wealth and mindset building declarations inside of the, Increase Academy).

If you had a winning purebred show dog, would you feed it McDonald's? Probably not. You would take great care of it. You would feed it organic food and would provide top-notch training and health care. Now, I am well aware you are not a wining purebred show dog, but you were bought for a price (the highest price ever paid), created to live life more abundantly, and expected to give account for ALL the gifts and talents given to you.

> *Beloved, I wish above all things that thou*
> *mayest prosper and be in health, even as thy*
> *soul prospereth.*
> *3 John 2:1 KJV*

It is my prayer you enjoy the book. Let it penetrate the recesses of your mind and soul until you come to a place where you choose wealth in EVERY area of your life.

With love,
Dr. Jeffery Chapman, Sr.

WHO IS THIS BOOK FOR?

He came to His own, and those who were His
own did not receive Him.
John 1:11 NASB

I have been excited about writing this book for a very long time and initially wanted to dedicate this book to God's people only, but I am well aware that not every Christian wants to or can even accept a life of abundance (at least right now). That is when I realized I did not have to limit how God wanted to use this book to bring wealth to others, which is great, but **He also wants everyone not to perish...**

For God so loved the world, that he gave his
only begotten Son, that whosoever believeth in
him should not perish, but have everlasting life.
John 3:16 KJV

So, if you are not a believer yet, but want to level up in EVERY area of your life, this book is for you.

See below the types of people this book is for:

- The motivated
- Self-help books enthusiasts

DR. JEFFERY CHAPMAN SR.

- Goal-oriented
- Afraid of wealth but ready to leave that fear behind
- Writes New Year's Resolutions
- Tired of barely making it
- Ready to thrive financially, in health, and spirituality too
- Multi-gifted and talented individuals that are not fully leveraging those gifts
- Those ready to re-educate themselves when it comes to wealth
- Meditation and visualization fans (Yep, I have scriptures for that too)
- Ready to elevate/for more
- The ones scared of their next level because they don't know what that looks like...yet
- Faith-driven walkers
- Magnetic and positive
- People that look at failure as another opportunity to try again
- And those bold enough to liberally declare the name of Jesus and God's promises over EVERY area of their lives.

Exciting, right? Did you see yourself in one or many of the categories above? I sure hope so. When my wife and I started our ministry 18-years ago we thought we had been called to "the hood", unfortunately, the kind of preaching I was doing was not received. Not because they hated it but because they were not familiar with it. They were able to receive food, clothes and financial help from us, but the teaching to leave their current circumstances behind they could not accept.

Eventually we had to move our church's location; we stopped fighting for and trying to lift up people that were not ready to elevate. The moment we moved to the North Side our church doubled in size. We continue to pray for them and who knows, maybe this book will make it to their hands and eventually, their hearts.

As you read this book you will soon realize that some people in your inner circle will not be able to come to your next level with you; their current mindset won't let them. This is why the prophet Amos said:

Do two people walk hand in hand if they aren't
going to the same place?
Amos 3:3 MSG

You can always pray for God to change their mindset and to remove the low thinking that has kept them bound and stuck all these years, but NEVER delay your own deliverance and blessings waiting for them to catch up with you. Their journey will start when they are good and ready, you however, MUST keep moving forward towards your calling and higher thinking.

Yes, you are embarking on a new journey, but remember:

This season might be unknown to you, but it is NOT unknown to Him.

DR. JEFFERY CHAPMAN SR.

DEBUNKING THE MYTH: WHAT IS WEALTH?

——————————— Many believe that wealth is having lots of money, but that is not a complete definition of wealth. I can see how many would think that especially when the only definitions provided by the Merriam Webster Dictionary are:

- The abundance of valuable material possessions or resources
- Abundant supply
- All property that has a money value or an exchangeable value
- All material objects that have economic utility

If that is all there is to wealth, I would not want to have ANY part of it. My God talks about wealth that encompasses EVERY area of my life. Let me explain further. You cannot tell me you are wealthy if your soul is not prospering, your body and health are falling apart, and you are continually speaking negativity.

Wealth: A genuinely wealthy person – from a holistic, God-centric point – Has abundance in material possessions, faith and resources as well as:

- Is healthy (both mentally and physically)
- Has a clear understanding of speaking life over their family and themselves – their speech is never hateful, defeated or limited
- Keeps a positive outlook in life and their future
- Is always open to new opportunities and possibilities
- Diligently takes care of their body by carefully and deliberately choosing meals that nourish their body
- Carefully choosing what they listen to or watch

DR. JEFFERY CHAPMAN SR.

- Frequently exercises and cultivates relationships that help them grow and make a difference in the world
- Uses wisdom to manage ALL the gifts and blessings the Lord has given him/ her

Now can you see how the above list is more comprehensive and makes more sense than the limited definition I shared with you before? After all, how can someone be genuinely wealthy if they don't know the value of ALL the gifts God has bestowed upon them?

Yes, the Bible mentions in 1 Timothy 6:9-10 that the love of money is the root of all evil (this scripture has long been abused and misinterpreted by well-meaning preachers), but let me show you an expanded version of this scripture:

"But if it's only money these leaders are after, they'll self-destruct in no time. Lust for money brings trouble and nothing but trouble. Going down that path, some lose their footing in the faith

Notice how The Message Bible expands on the real problem with "marrying money" or making it one's source. Regardless of how wealthy we may be, our provider is, and our faith should always be in God. Money comes and goes, but God has been and will always be. Besides, God has been using wealthy people to bless His people since the beginning of time.

I do not know if you are aware, but there are quite a few wealthy people mentioned in the Bible. Here is a partial list:

- Abraham
- Ananias and Sapphira
- Aquila and Priscilla
- Boaz
- Cornelius
- David
- Dorcas
- Ethiopian Treasurer
- Isaac

- Jacob
- Jason
- Joseph
- Joseph of Arimathea
- Joseph, called Barnabas
- Lydia
- Mnason of Cyprus
- Nicodemus
- Philemon
- Rich Young Ruler
- Sergius Paulus
- Simon the Sorcerer
- Solomon
- Women supporters of Christ
- Zacchaeus

Many of these people did great things for God's people with their wealth; just as today, there are many Christians that are TRULY wealthy and use their resources to bless others.

Take, for example, Bill Gates. According to Wikipedia, he is the 2nd wealthiest person in the world with a net worth of $90 billion US dollars. According to a Rolling Stone interview Bill Gates said the following about his faith:

"The moral systems of religion, I think, are super important. We've raised our kids in a religious way; they've gone to the Catholic church that Melinda goes to and I participate in. I've been very lucky, and therefore I owe it to try and reduce the inequity in the world. And that's kind of a religious belief. I mean, it's at least a moral belief."

I am not attesting or denying Bill Gates' faith, but I use him as an example of someone very wealthy that is using his financial position to make the world a better place. The article also mentions that he appears to be on a course to give away 99.96% of his wealth.

Bill Gates and his wife, Melinda, are very active in the Melinda and Bill Gates Foundation, and many other philanthropic organizations. Wouldn't it be amazing if more of God's children were in such a position to help developing countries, and in times of natural disasters and terrorist attacks?

My family and church are big on giving because God has been extremely generous with us and still, we do not love or chase after money. However, we do leverage money for God's Kingdom and for the expansion of the Gospel. Let me give you another example. When Jesus was here on earth, He told the disciples He was leaving because He needed to prepare a place for them.

> *In My Father's house are many dwelling places; if it were not so, I would have told you; for I go to prepare a place for you.*
> *John 14:2 NASB*

Do you know what that place looks like? The Bible describes it in detail in the book of Revelation 21:10-21 NASB

> *And he carried me away in the Spirit to a great and high mountain, and showed me the holy city, Jerusalem, coming down out of heaven from God, 11 having the glory of God. Her brilliance was like a very costly stone, as a stone of crystal-clear jasper.*

12 It had a great and high wall, with twelve gates, and at the gates twelve angels; and names were written on them, which are the names of the twelve tribes of the sons of Israel.

13 There were three gates on the east and three gates on the north and three gates on the south and three gates on the west.

14 And the wall of the city had twelve foundation stones, and on them were the twelve names of the twelve apostles of the Lamb.

15 The one who spoke with me had a gold measuring rod to measure the city, and its gates and its wall.

16 The city is laid out as a square, and its length is as great as the width; and he measured the city with the rod, fifteen hundred miles; its length and width and height are equal.

17 And he measured its wall, seventy-two yards, according to human measurements, which are also angelic measurements.

18 The material of the wall was jasper; and the city was pure gold, like clear glass.

19 The foundation stones of the city wall were adorned with every kind of precious stone. The first foundation stone was jasper; the second, sapphire; the third, chalcedony; the fourth, emerald;

20 the fifth, sardonyx; the sixth, sardius; the seventh, chrysolite; the eighth, beryl; the ninth, topaz; the tenth, chrysoprase; the eleventh, jacinth; the twelfth, amethyst.

21 And the twelve gates were twelve pearls; each one of the gates was a single pearl. And the street of the city was pure gold, like transparent glass.

I do not know about you, but that place sounds like the most whimsical city ever. It does not seem Jesus has an issue with wealth or the more beautiful things in life. He does, however, mind when we replace Him - our Lord and Savior – and put money in His place.

Real wealth is understanding that everything on this earth was created by and belongs to God. Real wealth is knowing that ALL our needs can be met when we trust God with all our might; and that trust, gives us leverage to use our gifts and talents with the liberty and dominion the Lord has given to us. That, my friend, is the kind of wealth we can aspire to in this life.

You might be VERY excited to be reading this book because you are ready to embrace wealth in EVERY area of your life, but don't forget about your negative Joe and Nelly friends. Share the book with them because they need to know ALL of this is available to them as well.

Keep reading and learn how you too can become a genuinely wealthy son or daughter of the Most High God.

2

THE EXPOSURE: WHERE IT ALL BEGAN

MY STORY:

I want to share my story with you because I want you to see where my mindset of increase began. It was modeled by my parents every day. They preached it AND lived it. It was not until I was older that I learned others did not think the same. Maybe you did not have the kind of childhood I had. That cannot be helped, I hope that by reading my family's story you can see and identify the traits of God's kingdom and wealth mentality.

First of all, my childhood was great, a very positive one. Many of the principles I learned while growing up I still use today. My upbringing was very - how can I put it - very Huxtable-like (per The Cosby TV show). We were the original middle-class family back in the sixties.

My parents grew up poor, but they wanted better for themselves and their kids. Even before they married, they both made vows to themselves: to have a better life when they grew up.

We grew up in a black neighborhood, where everyone was there for each other; the spirit of unity was all around us. We lived in a lovely area where everyone else was also a homeowner, and both parents worked outside the home.

My dad grew up on a farm. His grandfather raised him because his mom died when he was nine years old. He said to himself, "I do not want to be a farmer."

As a child, my mom grew up in a modest house, but it was not clean, so she told herself, "when I grow up, I will live in a house that will always be clean. I am not going to live like this; I am going to have something to call my own."

Both my parents had the same mentality even before they got married which was, "We will not live how we grew up." The same mindset was instilled in us, their kids. They demonstrated that to us every day. They would tell us, "This is how you enjoy nice things; how you celebrate life."

The funny thing is that I know God allowed me to enjoy such a pleasant childhood and developed my Kingdom mindset for the people I would pastor, and eventually, to those reading this book like you are doing right now.

At this point, you might be thinking, "Good for you Dr. Chapman. You lived in such a nice neighborhood, and your parents were great, but that was not my upbringing; I wasn't so lucky. No wonder you turned out the way you did."

I can almost hear the frustration in your voice, but I can tell you that growing up in such idyllic circumstances do not warrant a rosy future. I have close relatives that were afforded very similar conditions but still did not develop the same appetite or hunger for better in their lives. This book, my story, can be the catalyst you can use to catapult you to the next level of thinking for which God created you. Does that make sense? Back to my story.

MY MOM

My mom was totally over the top. My dad was as calm as they come. So, he just gave my mom leeway to be herself and decorate the house as she saw fit.

My mom was a sharp dresser and wore designer clothes. Yes, they had boutiques in the country back in the sixties....no Gucci bags and the like, but still, there was luxury shopping available. Her decorating skills were over the top as was her famous baking.

My mother knew how to go "over the top'" when it came to anything really, especially decorating. She could make something out of nothing; to make it shine like nothing else. I particularly remember a light she made at Christmastime, which was built in such a way that it drew other people in....to see the light. That reminds me of how Jesus asked His followers to let their lights shine brightly before all men so that they could witness their best works and glorify God. I can proudly say my mother gave only the best of herself in everything she did; a pure light to all.

She could even take a can of Tuna, put a light in it, and have it shine into the house transforming it into something magnificent. Let me remind you this was in the sixties; no one else was using lights to shine in their home. The woman was innovative too. My mom loved to shop and laugh, and she was very hospitable.

We had birthday parties, and because we lived in such a tight-knit neighborhood, we would invite all the kids to celebrate with us. We had the traditional cake, hats, clowns, and all kinds of other birthday paraphernalia. Everything was a celebration. It did not matter which holiday, Easter, Christmas, Thanksgiving, birthdays, whatever it was, it was going to be a celebration. It was not just about recognizing the day; the point was to make it over the top; to celebrate life.

Remember what I said earlier about still using many of the lessons I learned growing up in my everyday life? Guess what we do at Raleigh North? We celebrate everything at church. We have full on graduation ceremonies from preschool to college. We don't care how old the students are. We give them gowns, and we celebrate. We have parties and feed everybody; that's what we do at our church.

Celebrating life was normal; that was my entire childhood. I didn't realize this wasn't everyone's normal until we moved to a different city when I was older.

When I was ten years old, we moved to another neighborhood. My dad worked for the telephone company, and he was transferred to another city. Now, working for the telephone company was a BIG-TIME job back in the day. People didn't quit those jobs; they would only leave when they retired. It was not like it is today, with people quickly changing jobs as often as they change their minds. There were not as many choices as we have today and there were many benefits to staying with a company for a long time, like a pension or retirement account.

The new city we moved to was very distinct with whites on one side of town and blacks on the other side. It was not flat out segregation, but one could sense the divide. We moved to the white side because we were used to a particular type of living. My parents did not do this on purpose; they were just looking for a beautiful house for their family.

All my friends from school were from the projects, and I would drive by every morning. My mom would drop me off to school in the mornings on her way to the telephone company, and then I would walk back home in the afternoons. And that's when it dawned on me, "Everybody doesn't live the way we do."

Since we had moved to a smaller city, there were not many schools to choose from. Everyone went to the same school. Many of my friends from school lived in the projects, but I did not know that until I went to visit their houses and neighborhood. My friends were the ones to tell me I was rich; I had no idea. We were not rich; we were a middle-class black family. We were prosperous, clean and neat. Why did they think I was rich? Because our lifestyle was different from theirs, we lived in a house and on the other side of town with two parents. There was also the way we dressed, the type of cars my parents drove, our bikes. To me, we were an average American family that happened to be black.

When you see someone living better than you do and having better things than you, you might be tempted to set their level of living as a standard for yourself. Please don't do that. Yes, they might be doing better than you, but more than likely, God is showing you their life as a stepping stone and not a camping ground. Be inspired and motivated by their blessings, but don't stop there; keep going towards the level God has for you. His thoughts and plans for us are ALWAYS bigger and better than we can ever imagine. Just like it says in:

Now to Him who can [carry out His purpose and] do superabundantly

more than all that we dare ask or think [infinitely beyond our greatest prayers, hopes, or dreams], according to His power that is at work within us,
Ephesians 3:20 AMP

My friends kept looking at me like I was different, but to me, that was my usual. Eventually they got over their perceived view of me, and we built great friendships; in fact, I am still friends with many of those kids today.

MY DAD

My dad worked as a supervisor at a telephone company which meant he was over a plant. That was a big job for an African American man back in the sixties. However, my dad did not see that job as unattainable to him. He went after what he wanted. He started at the bottom and worked his way up. He was very appreciative of the job because he was well acquainted with struggle and worked hard not to lose it.

He had a high education mentality; he pushed education on his kids. I think my dad drove it too far, but now I am glad he did. Everything was about getting good grades. My dad realized that back then education was the ticket, it was the key to a better life.

He instilled in my brother and I the following education philosophy, "This is how you're going to make it in life." My dad was a great provider; he displayed that in his lifestyle. I am a visual learner; I learn by what I see. You can tell me something, but I'd rather see how things operate. Don't tell me, show me.

My dad would take me to his alma mater, and even there, everything was pristine and neat. My dad displayed excellence, even silently, sometimes. The house had to be immaculate, almost like no one had ever lived there. It had to look like a model home.

My parents would argue from time to time as all grown-ups do, but they still protected their family and acted as a tight-knit unit. My childhood was divided into two cities that were as different as night and day. The first 11-years of my life were spent in a neighborhood that celebrated everything and everyone. It brings to mind the highly favorite 1990's movie, The Sandlot. In the movie, a kid moves into a small town, where everyone knows each other and is always out celebrating something together, be it a Fourth of July feast or a carnival ball. I grew up in a neighborhood similar to the one depicted in the movie; one that played together and celebrated each other. Things were done on a different level. It's merely something you don't see as much of today in most big cities, or American society as a whole, with its endless technology gadgets, busy deadlines, and other daily pressures.

Then we moved to the other city where everything "slowed down." We went from a big town to a small country town.

And that's how I became a teacher. From an early age, it was evident that teaching was my natural flow. Others would try to emulate me; I became a leader to them immediately. When we first moved to the small town, my new teachers saw my report card and because of my grades gave me preferential treatment.

Why? They thought giving me time and encouragement was a good investment.

Let me interrupt my story here and give a warning or disclaimer if you will. I have a healthy appreciation of who I am, and therefore, always speak in a positive light about who I am. My parents instilled that in me. They did not fill my head with the pervasive "fake humility" bologna. Instead, they taught me to own my gifts, to stand up for what I believed in, to respect others and treat them as I want to be treated. Throughout the book, I will share many of my accomplishments and triumphs, and since I know you might not be used to that kind of talk, I wanted to give you a heads up. Speaking life and highly of yourself (especially when done to encourage others is not bragging or getting too big for your britches), is not arrogance either, after all, my heavenly Father says far greater things about me.

Your eyes saw my substance, being
yet unformed. And in Your book they
all were written, The days fashioned
for me, When as yet there were none

of them. 17 How precious also are
Your thoughts to me, O God! How
great is the sum of them!
Psalm 139:16-17 NKJV

I invite you to try speaking of yourself as the proud child of the King. I promise you will get used to it soon enough. Just make sure your head does not get too big. Back to the story, other kids would gravitate towards me for different reasons - I was an athlete, a good dresser, and a good student. I was always a leader, but many of the kids from my previous neighborhood were leaders too, so my gift did not stand out. It was not until I moved to the new community that I began to stand out and was able to see the gift. Other people wanted me to be the leader, spokesman, or their representative, etc. I fought against that. All I wanted, instead, was to be a normal kid. I didn't want as much attention. Looking back, I can see how God used our move to show others, and myself, who I genuinely was. God will often uproot you from your comfort zone and will throw you in the deep end so you can develop the strength to swim in strange water and discover who you are. Growth may not feel great, but it is essential to becoming the person God created us to be.

I could say this gift was nurtured by both my parents. Why? Because I was always involved in sports and even though my parents had regular nine-to-five jobs they made time to be at all my games (some of the games were even at night). They also attended all my away games. The family was their focus, and it showed in their actions. It is easy to say, "I support you." But attending games and events that are important to the people you love ACTUALLY confirms that claim.

My parents were driven individuals. I think that is one of the main reasons they moved to that first neighborhood. Most of our neighbors were professionals too; very few wives stayed at home. My mother would drop us off at school in the morning, and then someone took care of us and the house when we got home from school.

EDUCATION

I think my dad just wanted us to be self-sufficient; whatever we chose to do he did not want us to start at the bottom. He wanted us to have access to the best opportunities so we could advance in life, and that's why I took my education seriously.

He wanted us to succeed; I know that for a fact. My Father wanted us to succeed and be productive citizens. I knew that because of what I was exposed to in the home and watching my parent's example; I wanted a particular lifestyle, and I knew a JOB could not support that. Does that make sense? I knew that at an early age. Television also had a role in how I wanted to live. The TV was a significant influence in my life, second only to my parents.

Why do I say TV influenced me so much? Because of the quality of the shows we watched. Mind you; there were only a few channels available back then; like three or four. I grew up watching Mutual of Omaha Wild Kingdom (Wild Kingdom) every Sunday. Have you heard of that particular show? Wild Kingdom came on before Disney every Sunday night. Every child at the time watched that show because there was nothing else on to watch.

When I was probably seven or eight years old, I told myself, "I'm going to go on a safari one day." Guess what? That dream just came to pass last year. TV instilled that dream and possibility in me; it wasn't my parents. The images and places I saw on TV were not a fantasy; those images and countries were options for me.

I always dreamed of having a big house with white columns because that is what I saw on TV. Why? Because it was a sign of success. The people in the shows we watched were successful, and that is something I wanted for myself. The TV was like a vision board for me, a moving vision board. I did not feel all of that was just available to them; that thought never even crossed my mind.

I always gravitated towards uplifting and educational shows. There may have been some negative scenes or characters, but I never saw them (my brain did not or could not register that). I remember a show I used to like, it was in black and white and set in the forties. I checked out their clothes, their style, their house and I listened to their speech. I took it all in. I wasn't looking at the black nanny they had. I wasn't looking at any of that. Consequently, as I was growing up in school, I was putting two and two together. I was saying to myself, "Someday I'm going to have the things I see today."

Even today, when I am watching a movie with my wife, we look at the decorations in the house and the clothes the actors wear. For example, the other day we were watching Tyler Perry's, Why Did I Get Married Movie. We were looking at where they went; the lodge that they stayed in, and the clothes. We were watching everything in this movie. We looked at all the details and the effort they put into making sure everything was just right.

I've already shared that one of the shows I grew up watching was Wild Kingdom; I also watched the Disney shows. We are talking about all the classics that kind of gave me the world. Around the world in 180 days, I saw the pyramids, the Great Wall of China and the Caribbean. I saw all of these things and my mind was entirely overtaken by it all. In my teen years, I gravitated towards Elvis Presley's movies, not because of the singing but because of the adventures. The shows I grew up with are amongst the classics, and the sitcoms from the sixties/early seventies were clean and all-American dream kind of stuff.

Growing up my parents did not talk about college or what we would study. They just assumed we would go. Here's the crazy part, my brother and I didn't go to college immediately; both of us went to school a couple of years after high school.

My dad remarried (more on that later). He now has two more kids who are now my children's age. They are all doctors too. As you can see, he instilled the same love of education in them also.

My athletic abilities had something to do with my delaying college. From a very early age, I was very good at sports; extremely good. So, the focal point for me was professional football. I knew college encompassed that, but my primary goal was more centered on football. I recall thinking from an early age: "Football is what's going to give me the life I want." From that moment on my mindset shifted, and I was no longer so concerned about education. The funny thing is that without even knowing it, my dad helped facilitate that shift. He was at every game. He supported everything I did. My father continued to do this from Little League until the time I got hurt. Then, in ninth grade, I got bone cancer. That discovery is what turned my whole life upside down and eventually led me to where I am today.

Thankfully, we found the cancer early because of the pain in my back. Because I played football, I thought it was a football injury. Therefore, I didn't say anything. My chiropractor made the discovery. That's how college did not happen right after high school. The cancer was not the hardest part. However, I was utterly disappointed when the doctor said I couldn't play football anymore. Why was I so devasted? In my personal opinion, being athletic is a natural gift from God. There are good athletes, and there are great ones. By the time I was eight/nine years old, I was playing with older kids. They picked me to be on their team because I could play at their level.

I am sure my father was disappointed after he heard me say I did not want to go to school. After all, I had excellent grades because by the time I got in the fourth grade it was already sealed in me. I also had good studying habits. High school wasn't hard, and because my parents had high expectations, I knew I needed to do well in school. My family put the people around me to help facilitate my academic success.

I had to go through two years of radiation, chemotherapy and all that good stuff. I got so depressed about losing football that I told my dad that I didn't want to go to school anymore. And then, just like that, I was divinely healed; it was not the chemotherapy or the radiation. That healing is what allowed me to go into the military.

THE MILITARY

After dealing with all the cancer stuff, I was very depressed. I said dad, "I'm not going to go to college. I don't want to go to school just to go. I have been in advance classes since I was nine years old while playing football. That was my dream. To go to school right now just to go, I don't know if I could do it." I've been pushing all my life with education (both in sports and academics).

The funny thing is that in the military they do thorough physical exams, and still, I was accepted. That's a miracle because I had bone cancer; they don't let people in with pre-existing issues like that. My physical examination revealed nothing. Whatever records they checked they did not find anything. The marvelous blessing was that going to the military enhanced some of my other leadership qualities. I'm very neat so immediately even in boot camp they wanted me to be a squad leader. They singled me out because of how I cared for myself. All that stuff plays into what I do today. My wife says I had my calling before I started this church.

When in the military, you get to choose your job. The only way you don't is if your scores are so low that the only thing you can be is what it's called a grunt soldier. That's a foot soldier, a heavy artillery fighting soldier. When you go to the military, you have to take a test that measures your skill level. It's almost like SATs for the military. So, I just chose IT, and they were like, "Well, based on your scores you can choose these other paths," but I said no.

How that transpired was that my dad worked for the telephone company. He was in IT, and I said to myself, "I'm going to do the same thing my dad did." Still, the military kept insisting I pursue other subjects. That's when I said to myself, "I didn't skip college for this." When I got out of the military, I knew I would have my own company.

All of my jobs in the military were IT-related. Because of this, they put me in a special unit. They told me, "We'll train you to do special stuff because of your skill level." This afforded me opportunities to travel the world.

I didn't pick it; it chose me. All my childhood visions of traveling the world fell right in my hands. I got my IT going on, and I saw the world; things were coming together. I did four years of active duty and two years of inactive duty; for a total of six years.

A year into my military career, I got saved. My family was not saved, but they were religious. Now, don't get me wrong; we went to church every week. My family participated, but they had not been introduced to salvation. They were church-going people; they followed the Bible. However, we were not what anyone would call "born again." Until that first year in the military, I had never accepted Jesus as my Savior. I wanted to do so; I would ask others about it, but they couldn't tell me what it meant or how to do it.

The lifestyle of a church leader or being a pastor was not something I saw in my everyday life. I saw it from a distance. I saw it at the church I used to attend– only a Sunday morning thing. It was not a lifestyle practice I brought to the rest of my week.

However, in fourth grade, after our family had moved to a new city something happened. I had a divine intervention from God that caused me to quit cursing. I became religious, but I was not saved. What that means is that I began to observe, or practice outer practices other religious folks would follow, but my heart had not been changed yet. I told my brother one day, "Let's read the Bible." All those years went by, and still, I did not have a personal relationship with Jesus, until my first year in the military when I got saved. That first church experience was a foreshadow of who I would become today.

How and when did I get saved? Well, before that moment, my nanny had given me a book when I was eight or nine years old. She was an author and had written many books. She was on a PBS movie as well. She used to give my brother and I books as gifts. We still have a lot of the books she gifted us. One day she told me, "Read this book." However, I never did. Years later, the city park was showing a film based on the book my nanny had given me. I had just gotten married two weeks earlier, so I said to my new bride, "Let's go to the park and see this movie. I have the book, but I never read it."

My wife was already saved, but I did not know Jesus yet (we used to attend church services regularly, but that has nothing to do with one's salvation). We went to the park; we watched the movie, and it convicted me. Oh, my goodness, it convicted me. The name of the movie was, *The Late Great Planet Earth by Hal Lindsey*. We were walking back to the car, and somebody came and tapped me on the shoulder and asked if I knew Jesus. That's how it happened. I got saved right there in the park. The person that asked me and led me to Jesus belonged to the church that we ended up attending later on.

Please understand, before that day I didn't hear anything, and I did not feel called to minister either. I was religious, so I understood right and wrong and the things you need to do, which I thought were Christian attributes.

At this time, I was saved, and in the military; I ended up staying in the military for another 3-years. After that, the church we got involved with was an all-white church. There was only one black couple in that church besides us, but I knew that was the church we needed to attend. Not because of that but because of the level of teaching that I was receiving compared to what I was used to.

I was used to hearing preaching from the African-American perspective. At the new church, I was getting a word I could understand. It stroked something inside of me that pushed me to no longer be just a 'regular' Christian. I wanted everything God had for me. One day I prayed this bold prayer, "Lord, how can I get it? It isn't about materialism or anything like that; I just want to get closer to you." With that new mindset, I got called to preach about five to six years later. Notice I said called to preach, the calling to be a pastor did not come until much later.

When I ended my military career, I traveled doing the IT thing. I would still attend my old church, but I wasn't there as much because I was always moving. I would do three months at one place or a month in another place. I kept moving around.

By this time, we already had our oldest daughter, and I was just traveling a whole lot. The traveling is what made me get out of the military because my job was unique, and traveling was part of the job.

My wife is big on speaking what you want and putting it out in the air because I trained her; I trained her to be positive and look at the great things available to us. Consequently, when Shannon and Jeff, our children, were coming up my wife used to make comments like this, "I want a vacation home to enjoy with my grandkids. I want my grandkids to be exposed to this kind of living." Now that dream has come true; we bought a beach home. So, everything she spoke came to pass. She wanted this to be a typical lifestyle for them. My wife and I operate in that vein well; not over-the-top, not pushing it; we're just showing our fruit.

Do you like the fruit? Come a little closer so we can tell you how you can do it too, but we aren't going to force it down your throat either. I think we have gotten to an age, where we don't feel led to force anything on anyone (even if it is for their betterment). My wife likes to say, "People like to drain you, we aren't going there anymore. If you want it, we will help you. If not, that's cool too."

I think all the military training and all of the things my dad taught me, come together quite nicely with the subjects I deal with in my first book. It's already written, and everything; the premise of the book is, "Thinking, Speaking, & Living." The point is, you have to speak what you want because you have to go towards your words. Whether you want to or not, it's going to happen. Did you know that Nascar drivers are advised to not focus on the wall? Unsurprisingly new driver's primary focus is to not crash against the wall. They are so focused on the wall that inevitably they find themselves getting closer and closer to the wall. Instead, their instructors tell them to focus on the road ahead. The moral of the story? We move towards what we focus on; focus on what you want and watch your life turn around.

My wife and I live by that principle every day. Hence this book you are holding right now. Just more evidence that your lifestyle is based on how you think. Nobody keeps you down more than you; it's always you. What did the military do for me? It just enhanced everything that was going on in my life at that particular time, and I didn't even realize it.

Once I saw all the traveling I was doing, I realized I did not want that for my family. However, the church played a significant role in me not fulfilling my entrepreneurial dreams earlier. How? Simple, their mentality was, "Don't worry about owning a home, just rent; you don't need to own anything because it's all about Jesus. It's all about your spiritual life; besides, you should just focus on winning the world for Jesus. He's coming back tonight."

What did we do? Our mindset was on par with the Apostle Paul, as far as material things but at the same time, we knew that the blessings of God were for us. We knew that this was America and we knew their thinking was off, but we had respect for the Word and for the place where we were. We were already exposed to certain things before we came to this church. We were not "brainwashed" to believe that you shouldn't have anything, but, in a sense, we were. We were waiting for God to tell us what to do next.

We knew in the back of our minds that people still needed money to live. What we had was quality and very clean, but we were taught to own nothing. That kind of thinking held us back for a while. We did not get to the vision we used to have until we returned to North Carolina. My wife said to me, "When we get to North Carolina, I want a house."

The move was not only physical; it was a shift in mindset. Leaving Arizona also shifted us from the mindset, "Jesus is coming tomorrow so don't bother building for a rainy day."

The funny thing was that the main reason for leaving Arizona for North Carolina was to start a church. However, there were other benefits to moving back. We would be where our families were, and we would also be moving back to a familiar way of life and weather (which we missed). However, I did not start a church then. We ended up starting the church ten years later.

Are you wondering what I was doing for ten years? I began to sell furniture, and I did very well in that field. After two years I knew it was time to go; mainly because my only days off were Wednesdays and Thursdays – in the furniture business weekends are the biggest sales days. I had to work on Sundays, and it never allowed me to do what I came to North Carolina to do. It became a strain. I took the job because I needed the income (which was great), but then God started speaking to me, "You didn't come back for this."

A door opened up for IT, and I jumped into it as a temporary employee. Then they noticed that leadership gift again – our gifts will TRULY make room for us - and so I was hired as a full-time employee and then they started promoting me. That's how I began moving up the ladder. Mind you I had other jobs in Arizona. Many were humbling (I did some roofing for a while), but it was ALL part of my building process.

We got back to North Carolina, and life was moving a lot quicker than in Arizona. Our high school friends were already settled in their own lives and doing well. It was as if we had been left behind. Going back into my chosen field was my way of figuring out my place and my way.

I started as an installer of high-speed data cable, routers (in plain English: the behind the scene equipment that supports the jack you plug your computer into). I also installed category five, six and seven technology; I built all of the closets too. I was able to do a lot, and that's how I became a project manager. I was managing the most significant account in the company. One day the client came to me privately and said, "We like you, but we don't like your employer." I did not understand what they were trying to say at first, but then they said it a lot clearer, and I got it. "If you start your own company, we'll give you this whole account." I won't lie, it was a lot of money. The only issue was that I'm a loyalist and I did not know what I was going to do. I was not about to stab my employer in the back.

Six months went by, and the client came to me again, and I could tell they were not happy; they said to me, "If you don't do something, you aren't going to have a job here; we're just going to cut your whole company out." That got my attention quickly. One day I was an employee and the next day I was a business owner. And no, I did not get in any legal trouble with my former employer because remember, I started as a temporary employee, so no competes were signed when I was brought on board.

No, I did not betray my principles, did I forget to mention the company wanted to pull me off that contract anyway? I got pulled off alright, just not the way they were planning. Many employees were jealous and tried to undercut me and make me look bad. Some people in the company wanted me to head a massive project with one of the biggest home improvement companies in the U.S. while others wanted me to stay right where I was. I believe they were intimidated by my gifts and ability and in the end, God moved me swiftly and promoted me at the same time. The offer to start my own company met the perfect storm that was going on at work.

> *As for you, you meant evil against me, but God meant it for good in order to bring about this present outcome.*
> *Genesis 50:20a AMP*

What did I do? I worked the contract, grew my business and started expanding. I became known for being in hospital communications because the agreement we had was with a hospital (the biggest hospital in the area). When people got laid off, or people got fired from other hospitals and they needed IT help, they called me. So, I started serving the hospital grounds for the state of North Carolina. And that's how I ended up in hospital communication, which was very lucrative for my business.

But then I was reminded that the only reason why I came to North Carolina was to start a church. I was at the pinnacle of my business. I was making just about a million dollars a year in my business, but I was called to preach. I debated making the jump because I was still teaching every single week, but I wasn't a Pastor yet. The word was being preached, so I thought that need was being met. I had a company, and I assumed it was what God wanted me to do. After all, why would He bless me with the company? I was not struggling so His hand was on it and I was preaching every single week. I was meeting my preaching call, or so I thought.

I had not started a church yet, but I had three Jesus things going. I had a Bible study Friday night in the hood; I preached to the homeless on Sunday morning before I went to my church and I did prison ministry every other Friday night. So, I was teaching at least three times a week. The church I attended every Sunday, was where I served as an Associate Pastor. The other things I was doing came under the umbrella of that church as well.

I was an Associate Pastor, I was doing ministry outside of that, and I also had the business at the same time. I was happy doing it all. Then the Lord told me to start the church and let my business go.

I wanted my son to take over the business, but he was fourteen years old at the time. He was not even close to being ready for such an undertaking. What did I do? I did not drop my business right away, but I accepted the call to become a Pastor, so I started a church. With all that other stuff going on at the same time. I started a church in my house (in my living room). God said drop the business, but I didn't do it. It took me almost a-year-and-a-half to understand why He told me to do it. I didn't do it, and it caused me to get sick. My health deteriorated, and that's when I finally let the business go. I finally understood I was doing too much. Releasing the business was a hard decision because it was like my baby, but I always knew that a being pastor was going to happen; I just didn't know how or when it was going to materialize.

Even though I let go of the business our lifestyle did not change. The only thing that changed were our vacations. Money was never and has never been my focal point. I believe I developed that mentality because of the way I was raised. Money was something we did not worry about. I still have the same mindset today. Money is not for me to seek and worry about. It's not the focus at all; this is why the legacy you leave your kids is so important. They are paying attention and absorbing more than you know.

That is one of the reasons I decided to write this book because as people read, and go through the training, their mindset changes and their life changes; their kids are going to be raised having money. So, when they grow up, they will be not be tempted or driven to and fro by monetary gains because they grew up knowing how to manage and act around money.

I have three kids, two of which were raised in the Jesus movement. My youngest daughter was not. Let me tell you what that yielded. My older kids were, let's say, deprived of TV. Do you know what they did instead? They read.

Their appetite is quite different from their little sister's. She looks at her surroundings and says: "This is what's supposed to happen for me." That is my daughter's normal. We would be an average family by Arizona standards, but certainly NOT by North Carolina's rules.

She would say things like, "This is no big deal at all." Cars, money, trips. All of those things have always been available to her. My oldest kids would get excited about all of it because it was not normal to them.

My oldest daughter is brilliant, and when she moved back here to North Carolina, her friends picked on her, they would say, "You act so white." But what they did not know was that in Arizona there were NO Black people. ZERO. How else would she act? What am I trying to say? Because my two oldest children did not grow up with all the blessings we have now, they have a level of grind to them. I knew they would make it and be successful in life.

My oldest daughter got academic scholarships to go to school. My son felt that there was no way he could live up to her accomplishments and eventually realized college was not for him. However, he is still doing VERY well for himself. The oldest kids are three years apart. I can see that my lifestyle has affected them because I see how they do things now. But now they all understand the legacy, every last one of them.

And this is why it's so essential to develop the right money mindset as early as possible. It's not just for you; it's not just for you to be comfortable and to be able to have the nice things you desire; it's for the people that are watching – your family – because it will influence how they raise their kids.

Guess what? I didn't start where I am today with all the principles we have been discussing; I went through many turns to get here. I wasn't raised in it; it was not handed to me. I had to work to get these things. I had to employ strategic moves to get these things. And there had to be some abstinence from getting stuff if I could not afford it; the delays were necessary to get where I am now. I had to work because I had to go through those dips and the military took me to those dips. Why did I share all of that? Because I want to make sure you know I was not born with a silver spoon in my mouth. I had to do the work, the hard work required to shed old ideologies and cultural biases.

What we are doing in our church and throughout this book is modeling what it looks like, we are exposing God's people to another level. It truly makes a BIG difference. If people you are surrounded with are making money, then you are more than likely to make money as well. It's just like people say, "If you want to get in better shape, have friends that are in good shape, just by default you're going to be inspired and motivated to get in better shape too."

And that's why, even the church you attend regularly, will more than likely affect the growth or lack thereof in your finances.

THE SINGLE YEARS:

My mom died when I was 20-years old, but I still got to see my parent's marriage as an example of the type of relationship I wanted to have with my future wife.

I started to date the girl that eventually would become my wife in the 9th grade; she came into my life a year before I got sick. I was 14-years old. We were kids really; that's how she got to know my family so well. Her actions said a lot to me about her character. Another girl would have left me, but she stayed. Even though I was young, I already had an idea of the qualities I wanted my future wife to have (even back then I could see all those qualities in Sandie).

I have always been a planner, and everything has to make sense, and although I believed she was beautiful, that was not the first attribute that attracted me to her. I knew that if we started dating it would be a real relationship. I was an athlete and well known so I could have dated around, but that was and is not the type of man I am.

After I met Sandie, it wasn't just her beauty that got me; it was her down to earth conversation. She had her mom's make up; she was a hospitality queen – she could easily make anyone feel at home. She was a homemaker. She was already like this at 15-years old, and that caught my attention. I was already thinking about family life and values. I could already see that for us.

I was not trying to mess with a lot of girls, so I told myself, "I can see this relationship working out." I told her in the 11th grade, "You are going to be my wife." Can you believe she laughed? I don't blame her though, what 11th grader foreshadows his marriage? I would tell her she was going to be my wife, and she laughed because she was not thinking that far ahead, but I was. The funny thing was that she knew she was cute, but she did not see everything I saw in her. And the fact that she was not stuck in her looks got my attention even more.

One day I asked her, how come she did not end our relationship after I got sick? After all, it was apparent I was not going to be able to play football anymore. She said, "It just never crossed my mind. I knew you were going to be okay. I did not care about your football career. I was not thinking like that at all."

As I said earlier, I did not go to college right away. Instead, I went to the military. I was accepted no problem (even with my medical history), and the funny thing is that when they were processing me out, that's when they noticed I should never have made it in. That was part of God's miracle and purpose for my life.

All my friends went to college right out of high school, but I went into the military instead. I came home when my mom got sick. When all my friends heard my stories and saw my success, ALL of them dropped out of college and went into the military too. That's how much influence I had on their lives. I thought I was behind because I did not go to college right away, but because all my close friends decided to do the same thing, I saw I was right on time for God's plan for my life.

I came back because my mom got sick and was about to die, but I didn't know she was going to die. I ended up staying for the funeral and the services. My friends were going to colleges close by, and they said: "Man, you look good." And just like that, they all quit college, dropped out and joined the military. I think they did it because they saw the military clothes and the check. The sad reality is that the military was not their gifting or calling. It just wasn't their purpose.

I think most of them had a horrible time in the military. The reality is that it wasn't for my classmates; they should have stayed in school. You must know your lane and not try to take someone else's path; it won't work. But I digress, let's talk about the qualities I was looking for in a wife, even before I met Sandie. I knew God was going to use me and I needed to have the right helpmate. Many singles get stuck in the looks department, and that is not enough for a healthy and lasting relationship. I was looking for someone I could take care of, I wanted somebody that would facilitate my needs, and in return, I would give her everything I had.

I wanted the American dream; just like my parents had: a wife, children, and a home. I knew I was going to have that at a blessed level. I wanted the best for us. I was talking like this when I was 14-15-years old, but my wife was not thinking like that yet. I wasn't looking for someone to fight me or compete with me. I wasn't looking for any of that. I was looking for the life I saw on TV (with the eye of my mind).

I knew everyone could have that life, but not many tried. And there again I saw how God orchestrated that for me when I met her family; especially her parents. I could see it; anyone could see it. Plus, and this was VERY important to me; I needed to find someone I liked as a person. Yes, love was important, but above that, I needed to like and respect the person.

I know someone that married his high school sweetheart, but they never liked each other. I am still wondering, "Why did they do it?" They were not satisfied then, and they were not happy until they got divorced. The marriage was not a failure, because it was meeting their needs at the time. It was successful because they got what they needed and wanted out of it. The truth is that you marry what you need.

From the get-go, I was success driven, not money or wealth driven. I do not mind waiting for my turn. I knew Sandie, and I (and our families) had the same values, we did not have anything, but we were successful already. That was part of the getting married goal, to be success driven. The achievements came in increments, and we were both okay with that.

Sandie came with a great foundation, and I knew I could expose her to a next level mindset. She was open to it; we are different still but comparable in every way. We are of one accord.

Single people, please listen up, you are not going to find someone that is your identical twin in every way, that is not possible or healthy anyway. However, you must be of one accord where it counts. For example, my wife is very high energy, and I am not. What does that do for us? It allows us to balance each other out. She gives me some energy and I slow her down a bit. I wake up slowly, and my wife is fully awake from the moment she opens her eyes, the key is not making each other wrong because we are different.

MARRIAGE:

My wife and I like doing the same things, going to the same places; and so, we are always together. That produces a certain level of closeness. In the early days, I shared with her, "You don't have to work, you can stay at home. I like you being at home with the kids." She loved that. All of these years, coming home and finding everything is in place, food is cooked, it is as if we just built the ideal family model for us. It was such a blessing to know she was taking care of the family while I was supplying what I knew she liked and wanted.

I think we work because again, the principles of the Bible work in that area as well. We use the principles in marriage as well. You can use them in coaching, marriage counseling and every area of your life. The principals work and maturing together also helped us. We learned how to figure it out together. We talked out/ accepted each other's differences and taught each other how to understand the other. We did stuff like that from the beginning while realizing and accepting each other's personality. Learning about the types of characters helped enhance our relationship; it enabled us to grow and to make it through life's chaos. The other thing that helped is that we grew up together. We both knew we loved each other, and that we loved Jesus. We are human beings, and we know we are not perfect, but we know it will be okay because we are doing life together. If there's a bump in the road, the first thing we do is ask each other, "What are we going to do?

There has to be a foundation of course, and that foundation is confidence; Individual confidence. My wife had it, and so did I. Why? Because when you are confident, you don't desire to change the other person. If my wife were not confident, she could have said, "If you loved me you would be more high energy like me?" If I were not confident, I would say: "Why can't you be calmer like me? Instead, we are accepting of each other, as we are.

We are different people. We had no idea that there was a principle for that too. We used to say, "Oh my goodness, we get on each other's nerves so quickly." My wife and I tell those stories too, how we used to go through just as every average couple does. Why do we that? We tell people we went through a whole lot of stuff, so they won't have to go through it too. We then teach them what we have learned.

We keep it real, all the way real. Don't think, "Oh, they just turned out like this." Our marriage took some work, and we had to put some thought into it. I know I mentioned earlier that we grew up together, but we also took personality tests. One of my wife's realizations, "Oh, I get it now, you are not moody; you just appear to be moody because you are a perfectionist and you are going to keep going until whatever you are working on is perfect." We learned to appreciate each other's differences and learned to understand that God gave us unique personalities for a reason.

The results? We don't try to change each other's personality. What we do is try to adjust

DR. JEFFERY CHAPMAN SR.

to each other's personalities so that we can flow with each other. When we do that, I can flow with her and then, she can flow with me. For example, my wife might tell herself, "Okay, wait a minute. I know I'm a little high strung. I've got to calm myself down, and I should not judge my husband because he is quiet. When I think he should talk, I must remember he prefers to sit and think for a minute or two." What does that mean? It means that once you understand that who your partner is, has nothing to do with you, then you can take your mind off yourself and think of the other person instead. Why? Because you are confident enough to know within yourself that you are okay. You know that your God made you that way and so, "Let me see how I can calm myself down and find out what's going on in her life." We had to grow to this level, and because of that (at the time of this writing), we have been married for 35-years.

Whenever I see a power couple, and they got it going on; I tell myself, "I wish I could know their *real* story. I know they've been through some stuff, but because they got it right privately, God healed them privately, and they grew." And that's why I tell couples, "Get it right, or God is going to shout it from the housetop." Get it right, and you won't miss receiving the blessing. I always say, "Oh God, I've got to count my blessings."

He's tempering us for the blessing; some people cannot handle the blessing, and merely look the part. But I can look at people and tell who they really are. Whether they are a couple or an individual, they got a story. I know they've been through some stuff and they passed the test, and it made them stronger.

And that is what happened to us, my wife and me. We have been through a lot of stuff, but when we have a crisis, we say, "We are committed; we love each other, and we know where our confidence comes from." That confidence comes through Christ, and that prevents us from being co-dependent on each other.

You see it in Hollywood movies all the time when one person tells the other how they completed them because they are just the same. Nothing could be further from the truth, where is the growth in that? Our marriage, relationship, and story are going to help a lot of couples that at a glance may appear incomparable. They will learn that having different temperaments or personalities is entirely okay.

It is like the bride that admires a certain quality in her husband because it is so different from her, but then a few years later, the same trait gets on her nerves. But if she were to step back and look, she would see that the quality is good for her personally and for her growth. Even in a marriage, having the right next-level mindset makes a difference; you have to look at your spouse as your teacher and biggest growth supporter.

I always knew I wanted to talk about real relationships because other leaders are not talking about the truth. They want to imply that their marriage has always been perfect, and nothing ever happened. They try to pretend, "I woke up like this." Or "We woke up like this." That's not real. A lot can happen in 35-years. I tell the whole congregation, "Oh you've got to celebrate because we have been through a lot." And indeed, we celebrate our victory in our relationship. Because I could have left; we celebrate because we stuck it out. That's the growth; if we stay the same, there's no growth. You've got to grow. Husbands are human; they are not perfect. And the wives, they are not perfect either.

Couples, you've got to grow; hang in there because your reward is great. That's when you come back stronger than ever because you hung in there and everyone can see it.

I remember the time my wife and I saw a cute older black couple. They were so adorable together that we had to go over to say hello. We asked them how long they had been married. The husband told us, as he doted on his wife (you could tell he loved her and took good care of her) that they had been married for 60-years. My wife and I looked at each other because they looked amazing for people that had been around that long. We asked them how they did it. The husband replied without hesitation: "You gotta decide to stay until tomorrow. You say that every day. The name of the game is endurance. No matter how much crazy stuff life throws at you. After all, humiliation is motivation." My wife and I never forgot that couple.

TRAILBLAZERS IN THE BLACK COMMUNITY

My wife and I have often been called trailblazers, and what they meant by that is we were doing things that no one else was doing at the time.

We are not traditional. And we are non-denominational. We purposely didn't say we are this type of church or this other type of church. We deliberately kept the church community-centric and everything is different from any other church in the area. We wear pants; we sing cultural songs, like, pop songs. We are just different. We have children's church, and it's not just babysitting; we have a curriculum from Orange Conference. We have paid, trained and experienced staff. What am I saying? I am trying to show you that our church or operation is next level because our thinking is not conventional, our thinking is all about higher levels.

Most churches are denominational. When we started the ministry group, we were black-balled. It was like, "Why do we need another church? And why y'all?" I think that happened because everything we did was different. Even to the way we started the flow of the service; we questioned everything. "For example, why do they have to read Scripture before the preacher comes up? You don't have to do that." Stand up, sit down, stand up, and sit down. Why did we have to do that? Many pastors do things because they have always been done but have never stopped to question the status quo. There's nothing wrong or disrespectful with asking, to the contrary, asking questions opens doors of growth and innovation.

Our ministry was different because the Lord told us to restart the ministry. "Go back to the foundation. Basic Bible, not tradition or denomination." And that's what we started with. And guess what? By the time we started, people were coming to our church who had not been to church in years. Many hadn't been since they went away to college; they moved to college and just never went back. They didn't want to go to grandma's church, mama's church, or be there seven days a week either. We have timed services, we start on time, and we end on time. Many church people say, "Oh, the Holy Ghost, you can't control the Holy Ghost." It is true, we can't control it, but we can control the clock, though. So that's what I'm saying when I say we are not traditional. We have a set amount of time for our speakers. Everything's different because our thinking is different. Being different and going against the grain is not easy, but when you know who you are, other's opinions of you or what you are doing does not affect you.

We give a lot too. We don't collect three offerings either; we take just ONE offering (because efficiency is essential). We teach people about giving, and once they understand the principle, they give from a well-informed place. Everything we have in our building is excellent; we do not stand for anything less. Our building is God's house, and we treat it as such.

Never forget this, "Your surroundings affect your thinking. Clean and organize your house, car, and workspace. Surround yourself with things that inspire you to do and be better."

Another thing I cannot stand is fundraisers; I despise them. Why do we have to sell chicken plates every weekend? We tithe, offer gifts, and sometimes, do sacrificial giving. That's what we are called to do, and the Lord has blessed our obedience, so we don't have to beg or do fundraisers.

Looking back, I am glad we did not have any local pastor as friends; otherwise, they would have told us we were doing it all wrong. Of course, now that we are established and settled, we have many local pastors we call friends and even partners in the Kingdom. Why am I glad we started alone? Because God got the glory, and not me; I'm just a disciple. No one can say, "We did that, we supported them. They are here because of us." Everybody knows nobody supported us at first. We received zero support. So, in the end, God got the glory, and that's where it belongs.

Do you know when people began to say, "Oh, maybe they are onto something" about two years ago, maybe three years ago? We are 19-years old now, and just about 2-3 years ago we began to be taken seriously. However, we knew we were called and did not dwell in what others thought about us.

I get people coming by all the time, some of the pastors come by and say, "I like what you got going on here," but that's far in between. I think some of the older ones we started with, even before we started, those were the ones that were a little apprehensive about what we were doing. I think it was hard for them to break away from their traditional roots.

Three years ago we began planning to build another campus. We heard comments like, "Hold up. They went from that place to this place, and now they are building another place?" The funny thing is that I used to do the same thing. "Why are they starting a church? All these churches around here..." You reap what you sow, and that's why I understood their thinking. I didn't even get mad with them be-cause I used to say the same thing.

We were so focused on what God called us to do that we didn't have time to get mad at anybody. We decided we would not have Sunday night church; most churches in our area have Sunday night service, but we don't. We don't do weekly revivals either. We only have services on Sundays and Wednesdays. All through the week, there are different events, and various classes going on and that's enough. I told our members, "Y'all want to go to Sunday night service? Visit all these churches around here. Feel free to go visit." That's another thing, some pastors tell their members, "Don't go to other churches." I tell people, "Y'all, please feel free to go to other churches, especially when you are traveling, then you'd appreciate what you have here. When you go home and visit Mama's church you'll come back, and you'll be grateful for Raleigh North Christian Center."

We have never been insecure with people; never, even when we were in a community center. None of this is ours because they are God's people. I have no right to try to control them or keep them tied to this ministry. I believe and have seen the following over the years; your personality spills into everything you do. If someone is insecure, then they would think, "These are my members. This is my church. You cannot steal my people." Some people in ministry tell their members, "Don't even watch anyone else online or on social media." I have friends who were told, "Do not watch those people online and don't do church online either." Others choose to act like their members are not watching, but they are watching other services and preachers. They are watching and hearing what they need. You can't control people because they don't belong to you; they belong to God.

I'm just so beyond that type of stuff. I could not believe it; I was shocked to find out that pastors were worried. That discovery blew my mind. I said to myself, "What? Why would they be so insecure with us? We just started our ministry." If leaders don't deal with their personal issues and traumas, they are going to bring that to the ministry, and that's where people get 'church hurt.' But the truth is, it is not church hurt, its people hurt inside the church. That's unfortunate, but that is what's happening.

We did not go the traditional route when it came to the setup of our stage area either. We did not set up the stage like other churches; we followed our instincts.

Another thing we felt very strongly about was being available for the community, especially kids. Let the kids have fun; if you don't want them to go out on Halloween bring them to our church and call it Fall Fest. I want to give parents an alternative; I want them to feel welcomed, part of our community. The kids will be all right. You are okay; you went trick-or-treating, and nothing happened to you, right? It's not a big deal. God isn't even concerned with that. Many get stuck on that. He's not stuck on Halloween candy. Do you think God is going to stop your blessings because you got some Halloween candy? It's not that important. After all, people are dying and going to hell; people are plagued by poverty; people are sick. And saved people are wasting time on this? Get serious, people.

Other local pastors and friends would ask something like, "What do you think about

XYZ" And I would say, "I think nothing."
"What's your view on this issue or that issue?"
My answer inevitably is, "I don't care enough to
talk about it. I don't care whether they do it or
don't." That's what I tell them. Those answers
don't let them forget so they don't ask me in-
consequential questions like that anymore. Of
course, it gets a little awkward after that; then I
talk about the things we do care and do in our
church. We teach budgeting, tithing, Financial
Peace University, Crown Financial Ministry,
Divorce Care, Veterans Ministry, Healthy Lifestyle Ministry, and we also show our members
to give to other churches and ministries. Why
do we do all that? Because from the beginning I said I wanted to be different from other
churches.

One of my favorite ministries is the
Healthy Lifestyle Ministry. In that ministry we
do stuff like going to grocery stores; once we
had a farmer's market come to the campus. We
have also gone to a farmer's market in the villa.
Why? Because we care about our people's total
person, body, soul, and spirit. We have had a
walking group, bicycle group, and motorcycle

club. All because we are community-minded, and we are balanced. You do not put on Christianity. You take on Christianity. It's a lifestyle. People don't know how to be saved. Go to the wedding. It's okay. Go to the reception. It's okay. Go where the people are; that's what Jesus did. After all, what is the point of only hanging out with saved people all the time? They already have Jesus. Go where love and the Truth are needed.

We recently bought land down the street from our main campus; we are moving! The move will probably take place two to three years from now – but never the less, we are moving to a larger location. We are building a multi-purpose campus or community center if you will. The campus will have walking trails, basketball courts, soccer fields, organic gardens, classrooms, and all the amenities. Why? Because we are reaching the community. We also have Girl Scout troops; all of that is community balance. Taking your whole lifestyle into the world, and the marketplace; affecting everywhere you go and being able to relate to others that may not believe what you believe.

You should be able to connect to a Girl Scout. Be ready to talk to others by leveraging your healthy choices; be it a farmer's market, or via exercising.

We wanted our church to reflect us; the way we live our lives. Many of our members get new houses and cars when they join us. There's anointing here. Unfortunately, many times you see a pastor that's prospering but the congregation is not and therefore, the congregation isn't very happy with them. That is a horrible testimony. We want our members to reflect us. You can tell that under our Christ-based discipleship there is balance. We eat healthy food, go to the gym to work out. We do things in excellence: everything, work, ministry, and giving. We are always the first ones to give because we want to lead by example.

We give in ways our church can see and learn. What does that mean? That means that we make sure we reflect Jesus; like you want your kids to be like you; but if you don't want your kids to be like you, then you may need to make some changes. And that's why we let them see us together, my wife and I; we are not separate. We are a team. We run the church together; we minister together. We are one, and the two can't separate. Therefore, you have a secure and robust congregation. The congregation feels safe when they know that their pastors are confident.

USING BUSINESS PRINCIPLES TO BUILD THE CHURCH

What does that mean? It means that the church is a business. People don't like to look at it that way because they want to keep it "too" spiritual. What I mean by using business principles to build the church is that you have to be able to keep the facility operating on the level that you have envisioned it would operate. Let me give you as an example, the five-star restaurant Mirador, located at The Joule Hotel in Dallas, TX. I was sitting there one day, and the Lord showed me and said, "Now this is how the church is supposed to operate." He said, "The chef is the senior pastor. His executive chefs are the ministers. The servers are the deacons. The hostesses are the greeters." He then said, "Now, everything that this ship does, the level that he is producing on, it's going to be on the level of people's appetite. The facility, the ambiance of it is going to be part of it as well. So, we are living all these natural principles that are out there, and the church should reflect it at the same level. Thus, you will get a certain kind of people coming to your church based on what you produce and make available."

Also, we notice that many ministries do not have a good business head or foundation. They do not prosper; for example, their accounting department is nonexistent; the pastor does the church's books. Should we discuss staffing the church? These same pastors don't have a qualified staff or team in place either. I believe that happens because they make hiring decisions based on personal relationships, instead of skillset. That combination means the ministry doesn't prosper; it just cannot do well. I am not saying lack of operational capital is not real, but that part of the puzzle is not as important. The main issue is the spiritual mindset; it is often so religious that they feel they have to keep the books themselves (instead of paying a professional, or they don't have a long term/growth plan or organizational chart). All those things are and should be found in a stable business. The church prospers when it is run as a business.

I know some say, "You're too business minded; extremely business minded." I believe that structure or foundation is the key to building anything with a high level of effectiveness. They are correct by the way; I am a businessman (it is one of my God-given gifts). I will spend a lot of time on the foundation of something before I even start building on top of it. Do you know why? I understand the importance of having a solid foundation, and I also have some engineering training. I understand that when you are erecting a building of any size, the structure will have to be able to support what you are trying to build. That means you have to do a lot of calculations and measuring. As Sandie, my wife says, "You have to make sure the people are in place before you even start doing something."

Want to see such a model in real life? When Chick-fil-A decides they are going to open a franchise in a new location, they already have a plan and are taking applications at a close by restaurant. The new restaurant is not even built yet, but they are getting the staff together. Just in the same matter, the church should operate. You don't form a church as you go; there has to be planning and very methodical execution. What are you trying to build, and up to what level?

We know all about that too well, because when we began to grow, and we had to restructure our staff, that's when all hell broke loose because the current team was not happy and kept on saying, "Who are these people coming in to train us and tell us what to do?"

It was horrible, and it just got worse when my kids came on board. My daughter went to college for business finance. You can only imagine what happened when we tried to implement a corporate feel and style to our staffing; they were not happy about it.

We ended up firing every one of them over time because they could not or would not change. The staff didn't want a business mindset method. They wanted to gossip and began to say we were trying to run the church like a corporation. The funny thing is that I received that as a compliment. Because that meant the church was organized, structured and had room to grow. How can you have a church with a thousand members but only have two people on staff? That kind of thinking makes no sense in the business world; it just does not match a business model.

We had to sort all that mess out. The CEO or leader might be so comfortable that he can't see what is going on anymore. Sometimes it takes someone from the outside to say, "This is the way it's going down." Do you know what that is called? It is called business, and when churches get that business part right, they prosper. We had to learn this principle; it was a learning process. We learned as we went but all the while we were committed to implementing the new systems 100%. We had growing pains just like any corporation experiences when they go to a higher level. It comes with the territory. Certain processes you can take to your next level while others have to be eradicated as quickly as possible. When that happens, the staff has to understand, and, 'stay in their lane.' I believe when it comes to changes in the church and staff the following message should be communicated, "We hired you for XYZ job. We didn't hire you to be in charge or over the operation. Therefore, you won't know everything that is going on. And that's the way it should be." Why do I believe that? Because you have to think of the welfare of the church; the church belongs to God, and because of that you will have to give Him account of how you managed and cared for it.

Most people don't stay here, and that's fine. You don't want them to, but they need to go. Do you know why? Because if they can't get on with the program, they shouldn't be here lingering and spoiling other people.

"You are either supporting the vision
or supporting division."
– Saji Ijiyemi

These are things we had to learn along the way. It wasn't easy; it was difficult in a lot of areas. We experienced issues in many departments. But you know what? Again, we kept on moving, and God kept on blessing us. He has brought in quality people that can do the job at the level required. There is one principle I stand behind (and that's because we learned the hard way), I don't like to hire members of my church. We used to do that all the time; that's how we started. We started with internal people, and at first, they love you and say things like, "I will do this, and I will do that." But if they can't grow with you, they can't go with you. Why? Because they get too comfortable with you and your anointing.

I like that corporate structure because when you have a job, the corporation does not tell their staff their future plans or what is going on. But unfortunately, many church people tend to be too emmeshed in the church's affairs.

My wife and I added an entire section about this in our academy; we wanted to teach these principles so we could help people whose church might be struggling or not growing as fast as it should be growing. Or maybe they are thinking about starting at church; we want to open their eyes and tell them, "Oh yeah, we don't hire people that started with us from the beginning, and we don't tell them everything either." All those things we learned along the way and we desire to help other couples in ministry so they can start well.

From the beginning, you have to have volunteers. You can't afford to hire staff right away. Typically, your volunteers, if they stick around, become your employees. The issue is that the vision or plan may have shifted along the way, but the staff has to adapt or update their mindset. "Now you are a paid employee, and these are the requirements. Here is the scope of the work to be done. You can't do anything you want to do, and you can't say anything you want to say either." And there again comes that need to shift in thinking and mindset. If that person cannot flow with the new rules and regulations, then they have to be removed from their position. That's a hard thing to do, but it is necessary.

And that's the thing with teaching you see; I wish someone had taught us that because we had to learn by experience. People start feeling entitled, and they stop listening to your instructions. You tell them, "You can't do this." But they think the message is for other people and that your instructions don't apply to them. You have to be very careful when you are dealing with your church members and all your relationships. After all, everything IS a relationship. Why should you keep that in mind? Because they are going to feel entitled. Even in friendships, you better be careful because as soon as you say, "No you can't go or no you can't..." The relationship is going to change. What does that mean? Even before they become volunteers, the leaders or pastors should be evaluating and consider people's temperaments and attitudes from the beginning. Can this person grow, and can we avoid problems in the future? If the leaders would look at volunteers that way then when they can pay them, they won't have to fire them, as long as they picked the right volunteers from the get-go.

But leaders should not stop there; they should also add other elements, things they need to know and whatever you do, establish guidelines from the very beginning of the relationship. If they put these things in place for their volunteers or the people that eventually become employees, things will go smoothly, and they will also avoid major headaches down the line. It does not have to be complicated, something like this would suffice, "You are an employee now, and this is the criteria, these are the new rules. These are the new things you'll be doing...and this is what is expected of you."

It almost has to be a job before it's a job. There are organizations where not just anyone can be a volunteer. You have to apply, and then they interview you. After all of that, they have a meeting, in a boardroom or conference room with a hiring committee. There they decide who makes the team and who does not. The applications are discussed, and every member of the hiring committee has a chance to bring up their questions, concerns and thoughts. And then based on their findings, they decide to either bring the person on or to pass. If they choose to bring the person on, from the beginning, everyone is clear on the tasks or jobs the new person will perform. We developed this protocol because when we started the ministry, we did not interview volunteers and that caused a lot of headaches and avoidable issues down the line. That is why I tell pastors or people in ministry, from the beginning, interview your volunteers just like you never met them before, and don't forget to ask for references (asking is not enough, have someone check the references as well).

It has to be a privilege; because that's what it is. Many people think it's a given, that the mere act of applying means they are going to be a volunteer. I know at the beginning many churches are desperate for volunteers, so they'll take anybody and everyone. But pastors and ministries that are organized and have a plan in place will have volunteers lined up before they open their doors. The other consideration to keep in mind is the following; your volunteers will learn your process and systems, that changes things. Now, they are not just volunteering; they are actually in a mentoring program. Remind them, that is why they are not getting pay with money but with skills and mentoring. Never forget to teach what a privilege it is to be a volunteer, because it is. It's an honor to volunteer, and I do tell our volunteers, "It's an honor to serve." And I go hard like that because accessibility is an honor. When you volunteer, you get to come to places other people can't access. Others don't know what's going on and they don't see what takes place behind the scenes. And that's an honor.

Many experienced volunteers and church staff think you won't fire them because that has been their experience at other ministries. Not at Raleigh North. I have terminated people that needed to get fired. I would fire under-performing staff members, and still, some of our staff did not think they could get fired. And then I would say, "Oh, we are firing you too."

If they think anybody can be a volunteer, then they have no incentive to do a great job. If they know they can be replaced and could lose all the access and privileges - because people at churches love the access. Many volunteers enjoy saying, "As a volunteer, I have access to the first lady." - In our church, the staff knows the privilege can be lost very quickly.

I'm the kind of person that will fire someone and block their cell phone number afterwards. Because if they no longer have the position, then they lose the access. They can't text you whenever they want. They are blocked because the privilege is gone. I know some may find that practice hardcore, and that is why SO many pastors are burned out and exhausted. They have no boundaries and allow everyone else to control their schedule. Again, a corporation is not opened 24-7 and neither should the pastor's cell phone be. Even having access to the cell phone number, no everybody has to have the number either; that's part of the privilege that many volunteers and staff members take for granted. If you no longer work for us, that means you are getting blocked. All the way blocked.

It is imperative these conversations take place from the beginning, and it is also essential to discuss what the process would look like,

"This position gives you access to this…and when that time ends…," some pastors, leaders or churches time the access. Some staff members or volunteers mistakenly think the availability is forever, but that should not be the case.

Unfortunately, that's the church's mentality; they think they can walk all over you and still have access to you. Or, walk all over your wife and yet have access to you. My mentality is, "Nuh-uh, if you don't speak to me; don't try to circumvent the system by trying to speak to my wife." Our church knows that's my mindset. Once the access is lost the person cannot just check in on me. If the person needs something, they can call the church. And then that also spills to our personal life; the pastor's house does not have an open-door policy. Visitors can't stop by without an invitation or even know where the house is.

I know I spent a lot time in this section and that's because there is no manual for this kind of training for new pastors. I desire to protect you from a lot of headaches and pain down the road.

MINDSET:

You can tell me all kind of things because words are cheap, you can share all kinds of things, but can I see it? What is the evidence of you living the way you keep preaching? Our lifestyle and how we do everything should be something others can see and verify. Many don't realize our building is 8-years old. They come in and might report, "There is dust in x room, or something else is out of order." Our response is, every time, "We'll take care of it." If something does break, someone is going to be all over it in a flash. We don't let things stay broken; especially not on a Sunday or Wednesday; on those days, NOTHING will be out of order. For example, with a church this size with loads of people wanting or needing to use the bathroom, we cannot afford to have two stalls out of order. Our mindset is all about excellence. Our buildings must reflect that every single day. We don't want to preach one thing and have our actions and properties scream something completely different.

What is your mindset? Is it in alignment with what you say you want out of life? It is time you reconcile what you say you want with what you do and who you surround yourself with. If the mindset audit reveals discrepancies, then adjustments must be made. Unless you are happy with your current status quo, if you are, nothing needs to change. These are things to meditate on and then take action accordingly.

CHAPTER

4

THE TOOLS

I am excited to share with you the VERY tools, books, and resources I used to improve my wealth education and mindset.

SOME OF MY FAVORITE AUTHORS ARE:

→ Write out mine

Myles Munroe, John Maxwell, TD Jakes, Dr. Mike Murdock, those are some of the leaders that have influenced, encouraged my desire and hunger for excellence.

LEADERS AND MENTORS: —▷ *write mine out!*

Clifton Buckrham, Sr.

Apostle Michael Dudley

Aunt Dorothy Marsh (aka "Aunt Dot")

Jeff Fountain

I would recommend you read the books listed in this section and look up the above author/leaders; they taught me how to get along with theology and exposed me to the many levels of excellence available to me, my family and ministry. The beauty of all the books above is that you did not have to write them; all you have to do is apply the treasures found in them. It is the same with this book you are reading right now. Hopefully, you will also learn and apply its principles in your life, business/career and use them to pursue your God-size dreams.

Let me share a bit more about two people I listed above and tell you why they were SO influential in my life. The first one is Aunt Dot, and this is why. I have always been fond of my Aunt Dot. She only had a 6th grade education but she taught me about the power of words. She specifically modeled how to speak what I wanted, regardless of the situation in front of me. She influenced both me and Lady Chapman to speak positive, faith-filled words. This had a tremendous impact on our personal lives, the growth of our church, and the success of my businesses.

The other person that influenced me greatly is my former co-worker Jeff Fountain. He pushed and motivated me to go into business for myself. At the time, I was actually satisfied with working for someone else, but Jeff Fountain saw my potential (even when I couldn't see it within myself). Jeff further taught me the importance of surrounding oneself with people who will encourage you to go further in life and not settle for mediocrity. Maybe this is why I often ask my staff and church members when preaching, "Who's in your corner?" This principle is something I believe in very strongly and teach as often as I can at our church.

THE BOOKS:

As A Man Thinketh – Unbeknownst to me, this book made me realize that, "You produce what You Think." James Allen

Think Big: Unleashing Your Potential For Excellence Ben Carson, M.D.

The books I listed above are great, reading them will bless you for sure, but if you don't implement what you read/learn, your life will remain the same. One of my coaches shared that once a client told him, "Hey, I read Think and Grow Rich, and I'm still broke." My coach told him in response, "You have to re-read it. You read it, but it didn't take. Keep reading until you implement what you read, and it becomes second nature to you"

When I read that book and books along the same lines, I began to say to myself, "Okay. I am not where I want to be financially; I'm reading because I'm trying to get there. I'm reading this stuff, and I am so far away from it. It seems like it's going to takes decades before I can apply all I am learning." Now I look back over my life and cannot help but to marvel because it did not even take that long. Not that long at all. But back then it seemed so far away. The trick is to get started. The days and the years are going to go by anyway; if that is the case, then you might as well get started now. It is like getting out of debt, it might feel like it is impossible, but you have to get started by taking the first step towards financial freedom.

The book that started my mindset re-education is, As A Man Thinketh. Think Grow

Rich came later, years later. There's a Think Grow Rich: The Legacy Documentary on Amazon and iTunes. I would recommend you read the book first and then watch the documentary. You will like the book if you like learning through stories. One of my favorite stories is the one of Thomas Edison. You can watch a snippet of the documentary here: http://bit.ly/thomasedison-tgr The elevated mindset and quick thinking of a loving mother impacted one of the most brilliant minds of the 20th century.

Have you read Ben Carson's biography? Well, let me share this story from the book, Mr. Carson's mom was always looking for libraries to take her sons to. He never knew his mom couldn't even read. She would make her sons write reports and then present them to her. However, Mr. Carson did not know his mom could not understand what they had written. In the meantime, the boy's father was unfaithful and had another family. But the mother never said a negative word to the boys about their father. Mr. Carson didn't learn all this until he was a grown man. His mother chose to remain positive and eventually one of her son's became a neurosurgeon. Isn't this amazing? She had the right mindset. Who knows how she developed it; maybe she decided to live and not die? Either way, her family benefited significantly because of it. It's the power of being positive; it truly makes an enormous difference and impact. Even if you find yourself in a negative situation, refuse to give in to it.

MAGAZINES: Dwhite cut mine

I read magazines that match where I am and where I am going. These are some of my favorites:

The Robb Report
Travel & Leisure
Success Magazine

HOW TO EXPAND OUTSIDE OF YOUR COMFORT ZONE? CHANGE YOUR CURRENT BELIEF SYSTEM

I have always loved to travel, I have found it to be one of the fastest ways to learn next levels of thinking, wealth and wisdom. You need to surround yourself with people from other cultures. Why? Because everyone you meet knows something you don't know. Churches used to travel to other countries as a group, but they don't do it as often anymore. I want to bring travel to church again.

Yes, it is essential to share the Gospel, but a one size fits all approach does not work for all cultures or peoples. You can read about customs but imagine how powerful it would be to go to their environment and see how they operate? Some things cannot be read about but must be experienced.

My wife and I travel extensively, both for the refreshment of our souls and to learn from other cultures. We are always blessed, encouraged and enlightened by the concepts and principles we discover in our travels.

I love culture. And I always want to know about other people's traditions, how they think and how they do things. When I did start traveling, first of all, everything came together for me. Everything I had envisioned long ago began to come together. Imagine my level of excitement when I started to travel, and I finally saw countries and people I could only watch on TV or read about in books before.

We saw that the world is so much bigger than the United States of America. There's a big world outside of America or outside of your home town. I was in the military when I got to see Germany for the first time. I was pleasantly surprised to see how beautiful it was. I encourage you to go see it and experience the style; how they dress and how they carried themselves. Of course, don't forget about the food.

I love that travel has afforded me to experience and see many people and lifestyles around the world. It expanded my vision too, and everything that comes with it. Yes, I enjoyed getting to see unusual places, but part of my excitement was also flying to each place. Why? Because it was like a dream come true. As I'm thinking about it, it was almost like checking off my imaginary bucket list; I have accomplished this. When traveling, you never know what your trip may yield; I think back on those things all the time and remember them not just as trips, but more as adventures.

You learn so much about different people, things you didn't think possible. We went to South Africa, and I had no idea that's how people operated there; that trip gave me with the opportunity to change my mindset about many things.

When you travel outside your country you see some of the news or stories people tell about certain places are just not accurate. For example, I abstained from going to The Dominican Republic for a long time based on what one person told me years ago even though my wife and I go to the Caribbean all the time. The last island we visited was Jamaica. People told me stories about The Dominican Republic and when my wife and I visited we experienced the exact opposite of what that person told me. That is why you must travel and make your own conclusions. See it with your own eyes, because someone could have experienced an isolated incident and that one event could have tainted their entire trip and therefore their perception of the country or island.

Making friends is not hard for my wife and me. We made friends with our cab driver when we went to St. Thomas the first time. One of the great things about technology is that we always tell the people we meet to keep in touch with us and to watch our services via livestream. And since we do repeat trips, and go back to the same resorts, the staff always remembers us. I may not always remember them, but they recognize us every time we return. Such great memories, those trips have expanded my mind because I am such a visual learner. I am so glad I decided to travel and thinking back, I don't think I have ever gone anywhere that has disappointed me. Granted, the attitude in which I have approached those trips has something to do with it, because I know people that have gone to the same resorts, countries or islands and come back complaining about anything and everything.

Are all trips perfect? Of course, they are not, but the good always outweighs the bad and that's what I choose to remember. For example, we were traveling back to the United States from Aruba and going through customs; for some reason, they were harsh and strict with us. I kept my composure, followed all the instructions and by the end of the interaction they loved us. Their entire demeanor changed. They could not do enough to be kind and generous with us. We could have made the situation worse by arguing or being demanding, but we did not. We looked for the best in the moment, and that's what we got. The trip was too good to let that one incident ruin the whole thing.

CONFERENCES/TRAINING/PRINCIPLES

I would encourage you to attend a Leadership/Pastor's conference with great reviews/testimonials. But make sure to participate in events that are at the level you are and where you want to go. Don't attend meetings just because you can. Attend places where you know the material, and the attendees will elevate your thinking.

Crown Financial Ministries is a program we went through as a family and I would highly recommend you go through it as well. Financial Peace University is a program we offer to our members. I highly recommend anything to do with money management. Why? Because I think people do have money, they just don't know how to manage it.

BUILDING YOUR RESERVES (OTHERS MAY CALL IT AN EMERGENCY FUND OR RAINY-DAY FUND):

The fastest way to increase your reserves is by not spending more than you need to, even if you can. For example, even though my business was generating a lot of money, I still budgeted for our family to spend $50,000/year. As I began to get big pay-checks, I put them away in savings. Within three years, our savings account grew. If you get a raise, don't spend it. The same goes for income tax refunds or bonuses. Put all that extra money in your savings account and build your reserves.

I'm not sure if this is a church thing or just an African-American practice, but people don't save up for things. Instead, they wait until the last minute and then, surprise surprise, they don't have the money. For example, if you tell people there's a conference coming up six months from now, they don't plan for it, and then the convention/conference comes, and they choose to use their credit card, or they don't attend the conference. I like to teach people in our church; if we have an event coming up, registration only takes places when they make payment. If the deadline comes and goes and they did not register they cannot attend the event. I want to teach them and break those unhealthy patterns, procrastination, and their low thinking mindset. People buy what they want but beg for what need. For example, they might buy a new pair of shoes and then ask for help to pay the electric bill.

Budgeting recurring bills or expenses should not be hard; but unfortunately, people don't seem to be able to accumulate savings. The reason? They were never taught how to balance a budget. The consequences? Late fees, and those accumulate very quickly. Just go ahead and pay the bill the moment it arrives. Again, I am trying to break that habit by leading by example. Church services start on time, whether everyone is there or not. It does not matter; very quickly they learn when they miss a lot of the service. Very soon they begin to arrive a few minutes before the service is scheduled to start.

I know you might be reading this and thinking, "There's no way I can save extra pay-checks or refunds." But I am telling you, it is a habit like making your bed in the morning or brushing your teeth. The more and longer you do it the quicker you will develop the savings habits. You can even do it automatically, schedule it and have a savings and/or money market account ready for those funds. Creating a place for money to go is a great way to show God you expect Him to bless you and to train your mind that saving money is a natural and frequent activity you enjoy doing.

Do you know what having savings creates? It creates non-emergencies. Life happens every day; flat tires, something breaks at home or someone gets sick, and you have to pay a high co-pay or deductible; all that can happen in a slow month. Having a little savings cushion will eliminate all those 'emergencies.' All of a sudden, no matter what comes your way, you can handle it because you made provisions ahead of time.

Emergencies are stressful, let's say you have to service your car, but you don't have the money, pushing that service appointment to a later day will make things worse down the line. Why? Because you can blow your car's engine, that will undoubtedly cost you more than the oil change would have cost you, am I right?

I already mentioned having a savings and a money market account, right? But there are other things you can do to automate your savings. If your job allows you to automatically take money out your check and put it in a savings account, do it. Your tithes and your savings should come out just like the government takes their taxes, automatically. Then when you look at your check stub or statement, you can see how much you truly have available. You don't miss what came out if it comes out automatically and that way you won't be able to push your new habits back.

The reason why I suggest automatic savings is that you won't have to fight with yourself and go back and forth about saving. Setting up automatic savings removes all that unnecessary internal battle. Plus, you'll feel so good and have a sense of accomplishment when you can say, "I have been saving for six months straight." The feeling is astonishing and almost indescribable. Consistent savings builds up your self-esteem, and very soon you'll start feeling better about yourself, your possibilities and your future. You will find discipline and will power you did not even know you had before.

FAMILY VACATIONS:

Let's say a family wants to go on vacation, but they have no savings. Want to know my position on the matter? The family can't go on vacation this year. I suggest they let the rest of the family know as soon as possible. Ask everyone to sit down at the table and begin to plan a vacation for the following year. The whole family needs to be involved in vacation planning, and that includes savings and cutting unnecessary spending. They can do things like eating packed lunches to save for the vacation. For example, choosing to make coffee at the house and putting that $5 for Starbucks in the vacation savings can adds up very fast.

Let's say two people in the family go to Starbucks every day and spend $5.00 each (most people spend more than that if they add a pastry to their order). That means each person spends $35.00/week. If you were to annualize that you will see that each person is spending about $1,820. Multiplying that by two, $1,820 x 2 = $3,640.

Just by cutting daily coffees this family will be able to save over $3,000/year. I am willing to wager you did not know your coffee or snacks habit added up to so much, did you? Go through your bank statement and identify other areas you can cut back or eliminate. Going on a paid vacation is more enjoyable than going away thanks to Visa, Mastercard or American Express (who are more than happy to charge you upwards of 19% + to borrow their money). Numbers don't lie; think about that next time you are tempted to go on a credit card funded vacation.

Plan your spending, don't just go on vacation with a credit card, without planning how much you will spend. Eliminate your 'carte blanche/everything goes mentality.' Instead, find a resort that includes all meals. You can also take advantage of a Timeshare Vacation Exchange Program. There are programs out there that allow you to stay at their property if you agree to sit through one of their sales pitches. Go to the presentation, but don't buy though. Timeshares are expensive despite how convenient and cost effective the sales person may make them sound; there are so many hidden fees (maintenance, cleaning, you name it, there's a fee for it). And another down-side to owning a Timeshare, you cannot just use them when you want to. You have to be on someone else's schedule. However, the Time-share Vacation Exchange Program is an excel-lent vacation alternative until you can afford to vacation where you want to and debt free. The program works as follows – at least back when our family used to do it - you had to pay $30.00, listen to a 90-minute presentation, and that was it. When you are raising family, vaca-tions should be local and low-key, at least until you can afford nicer ones. Take the kids to the beach and save your money.

By taking advantage of this program my family got to stay in some great places. We would buy Pizza Hut for lunch and dinner sometimes; we would pack the food, go to the beach and have the best time. We did this for years. I know not everyone can deal with the pressure - those salespeople are good at their job - but we were of one accord and had the right mindset going in. We have heard the horror stories of people trying to get out of those timeshare "deals." Besides, I knew my wife wanted to have her own beach house one day, where her grandkids could stay in and grow up visiting.

Unfortunately, what I see people do is go on the vacation even though they cannot afford it. They charge it though they have no idea how it's going to be paid when the time away is over. Why? Because they want the gratification now and they are not disciplined to wait until they save enough to go on vacation debt free. They don't have a goal, are not focused and cannot say to themselves, "You know what? Oh no, I'm not using my credit card anymore. I am going to start saving for things ahead of time from now on."

GROCERY SHOPPING AND COOKING MEALS:

One of the many things I appreciate about my wife is how she takes care of our family. When our kids were younger, she went grocery shopping, and she cooked for us because we didn't eat out. Eating out was a treat reserved for special occasions. We didn't eat fast food; my wife cooked every meal. Everybody came home for dinner, and we ate together. When you buy groceries, your family is healthy. That's how you take care of your health because you know what ingredients you are using and putting in your food. And when you do that, not only are you saving money, but you are also creating positive memories for your family. You are saying, "I love you and I'm concerned about your health." Her hands are anointed, and as she prepared our food, she loved the entire family. Our kids could say, "Mommy cooked for us and we ate together at home." What a beautiful memory for them to have.

CHRISTMAS

Christmas was never stressful because we planned for it, after all, it comes around every year, so it was a line item on our budget. I know this is a touchy subject for a lot of people, especially if they have kids. But let me tell you what my wife and I used to do, of course, we bought the kids presents but more than that, we gave them the gift of quality time. Everything was about Christmas; Christmas breakfast, and decorating. Our focus was the family, and that's what made it special. The other thing that tends to make Christmas stressful is a false notion and self-imposed penance of buying gifts for everyone in the family (your auntie twice removed, the uncle you never see and the cousin that lives overseas). We stopped all of that and made Christmas fun with music, decorations, and cookies.

I know you might be wondering how we did it, right? How we got set free from the false gift-giving obligation and the stress? We just stopped buying presents for grown people, we just stopped. And just like that, we were free.

DR. JEFFERY CHAPMAN SR.

We then brought that concept to the church. We shared with them what we did in our home; we told them that we emphasize the people. The trick is to spend quality time with the people they love and stop trying to make people like them by buying presents. Listen, those people don't like you, and the $25.00 gift card from the candle shop won't make them like you either. Just let it go and save yourself the unnecessary trip to the mall and the money.

The way my wife and I raised our kids allowed us to celebrate the season without them asking for expensive gifts or brands. We celebrated the season, the whole holiday season, and we would tell them: "Okay kids, we are going to buy gifts, but we are telling you right now, you can't get everything you want. Jesus got three presents; He received three gifts. And just like sweet Jesus, you get three gifts, maximum." I know it may sound funny, but it built a strong foundation in them and discipline. They also learned that the season is about Jesus. We celebrate Jesus and maybe help them to get a gift for somebody else. We always gave in front of the kids when they were growing up;

we sent gifts to TV shows, preachers, and College Crusade people. We wanted our kids to see us giving and writing the checks. Let your kids see you give and that will remind them that the season is not about them; it's about Jesus. We also read the Christmas story. Every Christmas, we would read from the Bible before the kids got to open presents.

INVESTMENTS:

You should talk to someone that knows what they are doing. However, you should still educate yourself. Utilize tools from sites like Edward Jones and Morgan Stanley.

Something we teach here, and yes, it is fundamental, but it has to be taught, having a life insurance policy is vital. We learned that many of our early members did not have a life insurance policy or even knew they should have one. Do you know what that does? It puts all the responsibility on the church when someone dies. A life insurance policy should be a line item in your budget. The same goes for a will, I know those two things are basic, but for people that are not planners, they are not. Many people go along with life and decide they'll figure things out when they have to deal with situations, but then, it'll cost them much more than it would have cost them originally; and that is a waste of money and it adds unnecessary stress.

AT THE TABLE MEETINGS:

We did not call it meetings to the kids, but that is what they were. We talked about life, what was happening at school or their after-school activities. We would ask them, "What do you want for Christmas? We know we are celebrating Jesus, but, what do you want?" Asking those types of questions gave us insight and let us know where our family was.

My oldest daughter remembers quotes I used to say. The quotes were about making certain things a priority, and she told me she built her life around those quotes. Those At The Table Meetings helped her find her purpose and destiny.

You need exposure; exposure is invaluable. You have to be introduced to new things because often people get too comfortable with how they operate on a day-to-day basis that they continue to try the same things they have always tried. When you are introduced to something bigger and more significant than where you are, whether it's food, help with money, vacation, or whatever it might be, it gives you a different appetite and a different perspective.

You have to make up your mind as well. Tell yourself, "You know what? I'm not eating at Bojangle's just like I do all the time. I will try something different today." Try a new restaurant even if you think it's more expensive than your usual place. It all balances out. Let's say you decide to eat at a high-end restaurant just once a month, or you decide to make healthier meals at home. Guess what? You are not eating junk food regularly. If you were to add up your receipts at the end of the month, you would see that you spend just as much or more than your once a month high-end restaurant treat. Why am I suggesting you go to better or high-end restaurants once in a while? Because when you do so, you are exposed to different foods, people, conversations and environment. Once you start to see what's available for you; you will begin to change your spending and savings habits so you can graduate to your next level. You just have to start where you are. Tell yourself, "I'm going to try something different today. I am going to bake this fish instead of frying it." Make Google your best friend, Google recipes and follow them step by step until you can make them on your own and with your twists.

EXPOSURE:

Whatever area you are trying to go or see achievement in, you have to be either introduced to it or brought into it. Let me give you an example, for years I used to drive by the house I wanted. For years I used to go to sub-developments. Every year they used to showcase their million-dollar homes; with whatever was new and hot, fancy appliances, a barbershop in the house and everything. I submerged myself into that world, way before I even bought my first home.

When looking for a home to purchase, my wife and I always went to see the most high-end houses. I did not want to see any homes I could afford; I was going to see what was possible. I wanted to dream and be exposed to the next level. Want to see what's possible for you? Go outside of your neighborhood and drive to the one you want to live in one day. The same goes for restaurants, get out your neighborhood: Google five-star restaurants or linen cloth restaurants. Make a reservation and go, even if you can only order a couple of appetizers. One day you will be able to order the full five or seven-course meal.

Everything is out there for you or available to you to be exposed to. Typically, somebody has to introduce you to it. "Come go with me. I want to show you this; I want to show you that." Usually, if you already have an appetite for that thing or area the exposure it's going to ignite your desire for it and more than likely you are going to do the work necessary so you can achieve what you want.

Let me give you a practical example, when we visited the subdivisions, all the model homes had the builder's business cards. Do you know what I would do? I contacted several of them and began to ask questions. "I want a home like such model, and I'm interested in features ABCD. What do I need to have in place to build such a home?" Guess what? If you ask those type of questions, the builders are more than likely to give you the names of the institutions and everything you need to one day buy/build such a home. You may not have the resources or even the credit score required at that particular time, and that is okay. The big difference is that now you know what it takes to build the house of your dreams. You are no longer dreaming or wishing without knowledge. You are armed with all the tools and even can develop a plan to make your wish and desire come true.

You can follow this strategy in every area of your life. Take me for example; I'm interested in flying privately. What did I do? I went to the airport to inquire and find out what the options and requirements were to be able to fly privately. They were thrilled to see me and gave me all the information I needed. Why did I do that? Because a great friend dropped by and told me how amazing, convenient and time efficient it was to travel privately instead of commercially. This is how everything started "Hey, man, are you still traveling commercial, what are you doing? With all the money you spend flying commercially you could be traveling privately." What just happened? I was brought into another level. There's that exposure principle again.

Years ago, I went to a car dealership to buy a car, and I just had to ask about a silver Lexus. I could not help myself, so I asked, "How many people come in here to buy cars and pay cash for their car?" I was shocked by his response! He said more than 60% of buyers that come in pay cash for their cars. I could not believe it, but he was serious. I was thinking it was the exact opposite, that they were making monthly payments like most of the people I grew up with do. What did that conversation do for me? It exposed me to a car purchasing practice other people do, and it planted the seed in my mind. I said, "One day I am going to do just that. I'm going to do that for myself." And low and behold. Eventually, it came about. But I had to be brought in to that information and to believe it was possible for me as well.

You have to put yourself in an environment where you can be exposed. Typically, it does not happen on its own. Generally, if you already have that appetite, when someone mentions it, or you get in the vicinity of it you will gravitate towards it. And you might say, "Wow, I want to be here, I want to be a part of this. I feel great here. This feels normal to me."

I remember the first time we had non-fried fish. I said, "What in the world is this?!" I did not like it at all. But guess what? In time, I fell in love with it. Before I made the switch, I had no idea that fish tasted like fish. We were brought into this notion; it was not even intentional. It happened by default because the restaurant we went to for dinner did not serve fried fish. We were in Aruba at the time. My wife and I tried it and were pleasantly surprised to see how light and delicious it was. We felt great afterward too because the fish was not heavy at all. We didn't know we were supposed to have energy after we ate. We thought you were supposed to feel sleepy and often, bloated. The restaurant in Aruba changed our life by exposing us to a new way to eat and enjoy the food we already liked. That's what exposure can do for you.

Exposure does not mean everything comes all at once either. For example, before I began this church, I had already seen the internal structure of the actual building. I did all the leg work, tried to hunt some things down, and worked to get into a particular part of town. However, there was no physical building or location for me to go to at that specific time. I just collected ideas, clips and inspiration over the years. I have a vision board that I used to keep up in my home where I had posted things I wanted to achieve, and one of those things was the church. On the board, I had the building, the design, all the marvelous promises I believed God for.

Now I send my staff out to trips around America to be exposed to the kind of things we will build down the street in the new building. We are not copying or stealing, but rather, innovating and being inspired by new levels. It is amazing how seeing something great can spark new ideas and even inventions. When I send my staff on trips, I often tell them to look at different places or things, if possible, totally unrelated to a church or ministry. Once they return from their scouting trip, we put all their findings together and create something absolutely new, unique and entirely ours. I use that same principle in every area of my life.

CHILDREN'S CHURCH

Children are one of our ministry's big focus; we care about them. We make sure children are safe; we have a check-in system protocol. We have gathered essential information and put procedures in place; no one can pick up kids if they don't follow the protocol. We don't care who the person or member is, rules are rules. How did we put such a robust system in place? By visiting several ministries and piecing together a comprehensive children's church safety system.

Another area where we have made substantial changes is in the parking lot; we found that having parking attendants out in the parking lot directing people where to park instead of letting our members and visitors park their cars anywhere to be more efficient. Why? Because people did not know where to park and it got a bit chaotic at the end of service, but not anymore. Now we have staff in orange vests with flashlights directing and guiding people as they come in the building. But we did not come up with that system; we had to be brought into that. We don't have one parking lot attendant; we have a team of them. We also have designated areas for pick up and drop off. There is a protocol to follow. Is that excessive? We don't think so. It is organized and efficient. And guess what? It works. The system was not in place from the beginning, but with time we evolved and implemented. But I had to see it somewhere else because I am a visual learner.

Exposure works like the popular quote, 'When the student is ready, the teacher appears." If you want something and you are looking for it, you are going to find it. The mentality in our community is as follows; they want things brought to them instead of them going to get them (almost like a handout mindset). It is as if they were saying, "Wait, I have to work for it? Oh, never mind then." Let me give you an example when it came to this book; I had to make a decision. Here was the decision, "I need to take care of myself first. What does that require? Making or finding the time to write the book? Great, let's do that." I made that decision because sharing this message with you was that important to me.

However, I have learned that people do the exact opposite. When I started my first business, I had to invest in certain kind of tools up front. Because, I was well aware that by the time I landed an account, I would not have time to go out to locate what I needed; I had to have everything ready to go and at hand. Those principles just kind of carried over into what I do every day. See, I believe in investing in good ground/something good because it is going to yield something great as well. Even when people ask me about the kind of food I eat, many say that eating healthy is more expensive, when in actuality it's not. Because eating the wrong food is more than likely going to yield sickness and disease. Illness and disease are going to cost you; they are going to cost you high premiums, time and getting on medication that may damage other organs in your body. When you look at it from that perspective, eating clean is not expensive at all.

HOW TO BECOME A MAN/WOMAN, AND LEADER OF WEALTH? HOW DOES THAT HAPPEN?

The "how" is based on scripture found in Matthew 25:23 NIV:

> *"His master replied, 'Well done, good and faithful servant! You have been faithful with a few things; I will put you in charge of many things. Come and share your master's happiness!'*

If you can be faithful in the small things, God will put you in charge of even greater things, but, before that can happen, you must be faithful in your current season or situation.

We have to learn to hold wealth. To have wealth, you have to learn how to manage it, and it always starts on a small scale. If you are not a good manager when you have a little, then you cannot handle something greater. Often, we are asking God for more when we have not managed what we already have well. And do you know what that does? It takes our name off the list, the list of people to be promoted to have more.

We are bad managers; God looks at how we have handled or managed wealth in the past. Ask yourself the following question, 'What have I done up to this point?' If you have not maintained the lesser car, how in the world can you manage the more fabulous car? You can use that principle or question for every level, health or wealth. Don't think for a minute that God is going to see how you handle a lot of wealth before He has determined that you are ready. That is not how He works. He is a just God, a God of order. He has been testing you all along. And sadly, for many, they continue to fail the same test over and over, and that is why they are still broke, busted and disgusted. God is a good Father, a

you are going to spend the b...

if you have not been taught

properly.

Another principle I shar... younger couples when I give them advice, or coach them is, "Never chase wealth." Money is attracted to two things; money is attracted to vision and money is attracted to Mastery. Let's break that down; I have a vision. Here is my vision from way back in the day. I remember I said, "Lord, you gave me the gift to play football, and I was great at it, and that was my direction. It was taken away because of sickness and disease. What do I want? Lord, can you allow me to live a lifestyle like a professional football player without playing football?" I asked Him, and I completely forgot that, but He reminded me of that prayer later.

He reminded me when I got it that He gave me what I asked for. I had to have a big vision to ask that question. My vision has always been huge, significant and off the chain. Now, what vision does, it requires you to put ssary steps to achieve it. That's how ...cy operates as well. Prophecy does not ...ppen just because someone prophesies, or just because you read it. A prophecy should, line up to what the Word says about your life. Put things in place and then it will happen. When people say the prophecy didn't come to pass, I have to tell them, "Well that means you didn't line up with the Word."

Timing is everything, and often, it's not time yet. Many think, "A man or a woman of God said it, and if I sit here it's going to happen." That is the wrong way to think and look at it. The correct response should be. "The man or woman of God said it; now I am going to move to make it happen."

He has called us to have wealth, we all won't have it at the same level, but He said in John 10:10b EST.

*I came that they may have life and
have it abundantly.*

Guess what? That does not mean struggle. What does that mean? It means that you should line yourself up to what abundance looks like. The bottom line is that you have to be taught. At our church, we teach about everything. We teach about tithing and why you should tithe? We don't take an offering and call it a day, no, we explain the Biblical principles. "We tithe and here are the scriptures that go with it." Why? Because we don't want our people to do stuff out of routine and religion.

People think that tithing will make them financially abundant, but it doesn't. The Bible says if you tithe, He will keep the devourer away. The devourer is anything that will take from you, stuff breaking down or things you have to replace. Every time you get a raise, something always absorbs it. You get a promotion, and something always comes up, and that is why we have to put our money away. That is the devourer. It is the offerings that actually operate and bring abundance; it's not the tithe. That's why the New Testament very rarely mentions tithing. Why? Because it is already assumed that you know that and furthermore, practice it.

Here is how you get to your next lev-el, many don't know this because we are not taught this, and because of that then we are dis-appointed. Believers find themselves saying, "I am tithing, and I thought if I did..." But it takes more than that. And there again all of us have to lead by example. What do we do at our church? We show people; this is what we do. "You guys wonder why we have been blessed financially? That is because every December 31st, of EVERY year, for the last 35-years we set in motion what we want to see come into our financial life. We do this on December 31, New Year's Eve. We give an offering, and the offering is based on what we want to happen in the new year."

Our December 31st offering varies; let's say we want to be debt free, pay off a house or property, we have the following prayer/con-versation, "Lord, we are giving this offering for that house to be paid off." This next part is crit-ical; the offering has to be on the level of that thing you are giving the offering towards, in other words, I can't give $10.00 if the balance of what I am paying off is $25,000. Does that make sense? I have to give my best offering.

An Abel offering; it has to be a sacrifice. Why? Because I believe that God is going to do this for my family and me.

I didn't start out offering at high levels; my life has been about increments. One New Year's Eve I remember giving $100. God kept blessing me over the years, and my offerings kept growing as well. The question is, "How do you handle wealth? When you get it at a small level, do you do the right thing by it?" God is watching, and because you have done the right thing by it, your obedience is going to create more wealth.

And here's the other great thing about this principle, God is going to bring certain people into your life, people that operate on that level as well. They are going to want to bless you. Let me say that again; they are going to want to bless you.

> *For unto everyone that hath shall be*
> *given, and he shall have abundance:*
> *but from him, that hath not shall be*
> *taken away even that which he hath.*
> *Matthew 25:29 KJV*

I used to be very puzzled by that scripture, for decades. I kept thinking, "Life is not fair Lord. If someone does not have any, he needs help. Should not we give to that person?" But the Lord says no, because if you give to that one, it's already known that they're not going to manage it well. That's why they are broke. But if you give to the ones that do have, they have already proven that they can handle blessings well. They are going to produce more, therefore give it to the one who has more and not to the one that has less.

I call our church, The Church of Ballers. I have ballers coming into our church and the very first thing they want to do, they want to meet with me after one service. The guests want to meet because they see that we operate in a spirit of excellence and they are looking at me as someone they can invest in. Do you know what that looks like to the natural broke person? It seems like the already rich giving to the wealthy. They might even say, "Hey, what about us?" Do you know what I would ask? "When you had that $10.00 did you manage it? Or did you spend it?"

We have been telling many people for years to give offerings just like we do for years, but they don't do it. Do you know why? Because they don't plan for it. You have to plan to give that kind of money. It is not as easy as saying, "Wait, the Spirit hit me; let me give a next level offering." No, you have to plan for your next level offering.

We get asked all the time, "But, how do you guys do it? We start sowing into the new year. We end the year strong and start the new year strong. I remember the years we could only tithe about $15/week. We were faithful, never missed it; although we needed that money. We needed every dollar, but it never crossed our minds to take that money. You have to give it back to the Lord. Why? Because it's already His.

These are principles that have to be taught for people to understand that the abundance didn't come overnight. It came with consistent faithfulness and discipline over what God had given us. When He sees that you have been faithful, then He will provide you with more.

Why? Because you have proven to be faithful. Many see the glory but don't know the story; all they see is all this glory.

This is why only 1% of America operates in the millions. As you have seen through my teaching and stories, I am not teaching you get-rich-quick schemes. The Bible warns us to stay away from that,

> *Wealth from get-rich-quick schemes*
> *quickly disappears; wealth from hard*
> *work grows over time.*
> *Proverbs 13:11 NLT*

The key to wealth is how we handle it when you get it. Why do you think most people can't handle lottery money? They are not disciplined. It's impossible for them to manage so much money at once. They don't know what to do with it, and even worse, they have no idea about taxes. The last person that won the lottery in North Carolina won something like 1.8 Million Dollars. Out of that, they had to pay $600,000 in taxes. Unfortunately, lottery winners don't have as much money as they thought they had won. Still, if they don't know how to handle all that money, they will soon lose it as it says in Proverbs 21:20 KJV.

There is treasure to be desired and oil in the dwelling of the wise, but a foolish man spendeth it up.

I manage my finances by the following principle; if I spend $10,000, I need to put $10,000 back in my accounts before I spend any more money. I don't like to keep spending without replenishing what I have already invested or used. I don't just take out, take out and take out money. That does not work in the long run.

I implemented that principle in my life when I experienced four years of struggle. That's when I went from wealthy days to roofing days. But guess what? I was willing to be a roofer. I was willing to be a roofer, for two reasons. One was before, I was traveling too much, and I didn't want a job that would require me to be away from my family. Roofing was available, and it kept me close to home. Number two was the ministry; I had to be home to advance in my calling. At the end of the day I needed a job, roofing was available, and I did it. I had responsibilities and pride was not going to take care of them.

I tell people all the time, "You need a second job." I have worked at Dollar Tree before. I had a regular job and then I worked at Dollar Tree because we needed some money. If you don't want to be seen by anyone you know, you could get a 3rd shift job at McDonald's. They hire people to come in and change all the grease machines at night. That is an excellent job for people that need to handle their business. There are jobs out there; people have to be willing to work. To do what they have to do to take care of their families.

Now, there were other jobs offered, but I'd have to travel. And to be honest, I genuinely feel like that was a test. The Lord tested me. I think it had to do more with the ministry aspect than anything else. That season taught me so much about life. I think if it had not been for those tough years, I wouldn't be able to handle what I have today. In that season I grew closer to God. That was the strategic part of the plan of God for my life; so that I could grow in that area.

Everything we go through is for our growth and a testimony as well. When I am sharing the Word, I can say, "I have been a roofer, I have worked at Dollar Tree. Guess what? You can work there too." It is easy for people to look at the car I drive or the house I live in and make assumptions, but they don't know where I have been or my entire story.

MASTERY

You have to master something first for God to promote you. He does not promote mediocrity. Mastery means that before you get to the next grade, you've got to comprehend the one before. If you cannot master that grade, you cannot be promoted. When you graduate from a university or college, that automatically tells you that you can have the potential to make more money. Remember earlier when I said, that if you are making $10,000 and you manage that well then God will allow you to make more money later because you mastered that little bit well? It doesn't happen the other way around. It is true that people can stumble upon some money, but that does not mean it's going to last; many can't keep it. Why? Especially if they make enough money, what's going on? They didn't know how to master it. They never learned how to manage it. They didn't know how to do a budget and didn't know how to stay within said budget. They didn't plan for their vacation, and instead, they just went when they felt like it.

There is a deception that the enemy has used to move in and pushed people towards acquiring material stuff. You know that's the American dream, right, to buy stuff? The deception is, and sadly, many church people fall for it, "God blesses with income so we can go buy the house, the car, the property, and all the things. Those purchases are going to stretch us to get them, but He is going to bless us." Now the problems begin because they are so stretched out that they cannot give anymore. Why? Because they have used everything they had and put it towards the purchase(s). What happened? They have eliminated the one thing that caused them to get in the first place. What's the only logical solution? To cut back on the giving aspect of course, and what does that do? It cuts the lifeline or the blessings.

Again, going back to the American Dream, it is always about the next biggest thing. Yes, you could afford it, but just barely. The issue is that that you are no longer living in abundance; you are living in the get by mentality now. And that my friend, is not a pleasant place to be.

How do people get themselves into such tight spots? I believe it happens because they still don't take advantage of the budgeting and planning principles to buy a house. They buy it just because they can afford it. Remember I said, "Just because you can afford the house payment, that is not enough. You have to look at all the other expenses. The heat, water, taxes, and all the other utilities. Because if you don't, then you are going to be house broke." All the things I mentioned are part of being a good manager of what you have. Many people look prosperous, but they are still living paycheck to paycheck. Prosperity is being able to manage well and have some left over. We don't want to just look the part; we want to be the part.

Some people keep repeating the same lesson. Why? Because they have not gotten it yet. They go through the motions and are not learning. That just shows you what a good Father God is, He could let you prosper, but if He did, it would not be a blessing. He knows it's going to destroy you. You won't give Him the glory, and you can't teach your kids what you don't know.

When I teach about wealth, I love to use the story of Moses as a backdrop, as you know, he was raised in the palace, and he had all the finery of Egypt at his disposal. When God called him to be the leader, in his mind, he thought he was going to go from the palace, into another position in the same palace, but instead, he had to be taken to the desert for 40-years. He had to get himself together before he could get promoted. David and Joseph had to go through very similar processes.

Let me share this about singleness, that is the time for the person to work on themselves. To master themselves and then God would give them the relationship they so desire. But they've got to master singleness before they can get married, or be successful. In other words, you should aspire to become, single, complete and whole.

LEADERS OF WEALTH:

One of my greatest assets is discipline because it is something I was born with and I didn't have to start from scratch or grow into it; all I did was enhanced it. What do I mean? I know about delayed gratification; I understand and live by that principle. I'm not money driven; I am success driven. I can wait for things to materialize before I get them; I don't have to have it today. But I love the aspect of building it and working until it becomes a reality. That kind of work requires discipline.

I am a work first, play later kind of guy. People used to say, "Chapman, it's sunny out here; it's a nice day. Why are you in that office all day?" Do you know how I responded? "I am working this hard because I have a goal. When I'm teaching people, my stuff needs to be right and tight. I can sacrifice hanging out with you now because I know how I'll feel after it's all said and done. I am going to feel good because I gave my best." I'm disciplined. I'm disciplined in every area of my life. Sometimes I don't like it, but it's how I was born and how I was raised. Consequently, all the responsibilities and projects I juggle today seem like nothing to me.

When I was in the Jesus movement at the church I used to attend; they were extremely strict. That didn't bother me that much. It didn't start bothering me until I stopped going on tour with them. It only started bothering me because I went a long time without seeing ROI (Return on Investment). I was willing to make sacrifices, but I was expecting to see something in the future, but when that did not come, that just created bitterness and frustration in me. ROI does not have to be necessarily financial; it can be spiritual growth, knowledge or deeper relationships. I need to see growth. Because, as many smart people have said before, "If we are not growing, we are dying." Again, I am willing to sacrifice, but I also need to see a return. I am a patient man; I can wait. I'm not anxious; I don't need to rush a job or service if it's not complete. Everything in my life, personal and career-wise has been based on self-discipline.

When I went to school, I did not go to school to get a degree. I went to school because my wife called me one day and told me. "I heard about this course that is being offered at one of the local schools, and I think you would like it." It all started with one class. Do you know how long I stayed at that school? I ended up staying for 10-years. I came out with a doctorate, but I wasn't going for it. How did I do it? I took one class at a time. Before long, somebody said, "You can get your bachelor's degree here." It did not take me long to make the decision, after all, I was already there, and I loved their curriculum. I always thought school kept me sharp and I love learning. What is the point of this story? Discipline has always been an intricate piece of my success. Disorder causes me to be out of order. Disorder to me means your mind is muddled. If your mind is muddled, you can't think properly; and that means you can't think systematically to create or produce what you are trying to build.

If I am going to have a conversation with someone the room has to be calm, I can't be in a messy space. I can't work from a disorganized table or desk either. Why? It throws me off. People may call it OCD, I don't spend time thinking about labels, all I know is that it throws me off.

Let me give you another example; I let someone in my staff use my office today. The person is not neat, and I already know when I go back to the office is not going to be the way I left it. However, I'm a whole lot better than I used to be. I just let it go, it doesn't trigger me like it used to anymore. Nevertheless, if I'm going to conduct business, I have to have things in order. I just described discipline again.

If somebody wants to come in and speak to me; they have to have an appointment first, a meeting just does not happen on a whim. That might be how the other person operates, but that is not how I work. I manage my time and schedule important tasks. Why? Because time is a resource and it must be managed well.

Let's go back to the discipline principle; this principle is ingrained in me. I saw discipline in three generations of my family. I was born with it, raised with it and produced my businesses with it. When people ask me, "Why are you successful? What is the key to your success?" I always give them some generic answer. I can see the look of confusion and frustration on their faces because they always expect some revolutionary, out of the box answer. But I cannot help telling the person, "It's just discipline man, I have an 'I'm going to get it done kind of attitude." It was no different when it came to sports. When I was nine-years-old, I would get up at 6:00 am and do wind sprints down the street. I would go to the garage and lift weights. I did that when I was nine-years-old just for the game that particular day. You have to have a business sense to build some-thing great. Whether you are looking to have a business or not, you still have to use the same principles in every area of your life. Why? Be-cause at the end of the day your life **IS** a busi-ness.

Jesus operated as a businessman in everything He did. People want to keep Je-sus on the spiritual side, but He worked with a business mindset. The culture of the Jew-ish people is all about developing a business mindset. They do not turn over a business until the son is 30-years old. Junior can never be on the sign until he is mature enough, and at least 30-years-old. You need to understand something, that's why Jesus did not walk into His ministry until He was 30-years old.

In the Jewish culture, they don't believe a business should be handed down because someone is related, but by going through the process. "Can you hold on or wait long enough?" That was the problem with the prod-igal son in the Bible; he left before he was 30-years old. He should not have gotten the inheritance; which is why he squandered it. Why? Because he was not ready to handle or manage himself or the inheritance.

To produce at the level God calls us to create, which is at an abundant level, a business mindset has to be a prerequisite. That's why I told my son, "If you ever take any courses, make sure you concentrate on business; because it's the foundation of success."

If I knew this stuff when I was in high school, I would have concentrated on business prep courses. I would have paid close attention to the two following subjects. Number one, I would have done better in English. I could have paid a whole lot more attention. But I had no idea I was going to be using it quite this much in the future. It's so funny; it does not matter what field you are planning to concentrate on, no matter what you do, you are a storyteller.

Let me share something with you. I took zeros from seventh grade to twelfth-grade in persuasive speeches, because I could not talk in front of people. I was terrified. I became terrified because from kindergarten to second grade, my daddy made me stand in front of him and he gave me timetables and spelling words. He would tell me, "Spell this," and if I missed it, I got popped. It created in me a fear of talking to people. God had to break that fear when I was 24-years old when He called me. I said, "Lord, I'll do anything for you but preach." Those were my exact words. "I'd do anything, whatever you want me to do, I'd do; anything but preach." God has a funny way of helping us grow because everything I said I wouldn't do; that's what He called me to do.

The second subject I would concentrate is business. In the twelve grade my school offered Intro to Business or something like that. The advice I would give to people trying to get into business, "Take business classes as early and as soon as you can."

There are some great business books you should read if you are serious about business. Start with John Maxwell, read all his stuff; he's a leadership kind of guy. All or most of his books are about leadership, but with business principles. His writing and teaching style are very digestible. Miles Munroe also wrote great books but, John Maxwell goes into business a little deeper.

I didn't realize that I operate on principles, and I didn't know that the principles came from the Bible either.

When my wife and I attend conferences now, we make sure they pinpoint where we are trying to go. We no longer participate in general conferences. We are only interested in the ones that are specifically designed to help us grow in specific areas.

Now here's a difficult scripture, that kind of sums up a lot of what you have read in this book. The Bible says,

> *For everyone to whom much is given,*
> *from him much will be required.*
> *Luke 12:48b NKJV*

Everything I had learned in my upbringing, whether it was positive or negative served a purpose. God says, "I have invested in you, what is the return here? I allowed you to go through some good things and some bad ones as well. Now tell the story. Do not give the G-rated version either. When you tell the story, give them the whole thing, the good, the bad and the very ugly." Why is that so important? Because people, as I said earlier, look at successful people or pastors, and they just assume that everything is good, that they have their life together and everything has been easy for them. But God encourages us to tell the story, to share the real story.

I try to be as transparent as I possibly can when I preach and teach. I tell them the good, sad, exciting, heartbreaking and everything in between. I give them everything because that's what is required for them to feel normal. Because if I tell stories that make me look like I walk on air, the person listening might say, "But my life does not look like that. I've never walked on air. I can't ascend to where he is." I have no problem demystifying that myth. I am human just like everybody else. Life happens to me too. I realize now what God requires of me is to share the lessons I have learned;

whether I want to share or not. I'm called for such a time as this. And you, reading this book are called as well. The Bible says in 1 John 4:1a

Beloved, do not believe every spirit
but test the spirits to see whether they
are from God.

Make sure you test any word, advice or prophesy said to you. If it does not line up, pull away from it because it's going to lead down the wrong track. You must stay disciplined to the call. Don't veer. Don't go this way or that way. The get rich quick schemes are not the answer; that's called derailment/distraction because it gets in the way of your core principles.

If you are going the wrong way, you will feel a burden inside, telling you, "that's not it. That's not it." And then God might say, as He told me, "What did I call you to do when I brought you back to this place? Get back to it. What is it going to take? Line up to it. Am I not going to make you grow?" He will continue to tell you and might even make you dream at night. God, He has given me so much, and now He wants a return, that is why I wrote this book and the others I am working on. God is an investor. If He has invested in you, He's going to ask, like that nobleman that went away to receive a kingdom in Luke 19, "Where is my interest?" He asked his workers.

God didn't speed up the process. He gave me time. When He called me to do my pastoring, He said, "I gave you a business; it's not like I didn't give it to you." Here's the funny thing, when I went to Him and asked Him to give me the lifestyle of a football player but when that dream died with my cancer diagnosis, I thought the business was it. I thought the business was going to afford me the lifestyle I wanted, but all the business did was helped me fund the ministry.

For three years I used that money to fund the ministry. I bought the vans, the offering plates, the chairs; all of that was purchased with my money. That was the role of the business; to give me the money, but I didn't know that at the time. I remember telling God, "Lord, there is no way You're going to give me the life I want being a pastor." I was not aware of the level He was calling me to pastor until I saw it with my own eyes in other people. God said, "I need to pull out what I put inside of you. Are you ready to give it back? I don't care what you are doing? I want it right now."

My wife saw all this, way before I did because I was stuck looking at the current thing and it was hard to see the next thing. Now, here we are, helping other people elevate their thinking. Why? Because this is not taught in schools, at home and not at many churches either.

I know I have been called to share all of these with as MANY people as I can and a book is the FASTEST way to do JUST that.

7

READY TO INCREASE YOUR THINKING?

—————————— We did it. We got through ALL the stories, principles and teachings God put in my heart for you. Why do you think I shared SO many stories with you; Aside from the fact that I am a storyteller? I did that because I wanted to drive the principles home to you. I wanted to make sure you would see the caliber and height of the thoughts that brought me to where I am today. It was not easy, but I can tell you this, it has been worth it. You might forget the title of this book, you might even forget my name, but the stories, those will stay with you for a VERY long time.

Why did I spend SO much time talking about your thoughts? Because, the Bible does say,

For as he thinketh in his heart, so is he. Proverbs 23:7 KJV

Yes, your thoughts drive you or keep your life stuck in less than ideal circumstances, whether you are aware of it or not. I wrote this book to help you change the way you think and see yourself. I wanted to expose you to a new level of thinking and make you aware of a higher way of living that is VERY much available to those that want it.

Do you know that MANY people go without for lack of knowledge? Meaning that there are resources, programs and solutions that have been created for people just like them, but because they don't know about it, they often don't see their dreams come true. I know MANY people that aspire to do more. Aspiring entrepreneurs, writers, coaches, you name it, they remain in the aspiring stage because their current thinking does not allow them to see the many resources available to them. I don't want that to be you. You were created on purpose and with a purpose. I also know that you have been feeling this way for a VERY long time, and although I know this book has

DR. JEFFERY CHAPMAN SR.

been and will continue to be of great help and inspiration to you; I also know that more is necessary (more guidance, intentional stories, teaching, encouragement and impartation) to help you see yourself as God sees you and for you to break out of the shell that has held you hostage for far too long. How am I going to help you? You did not think I could just leave you half way through your transformation and elevation, right?

I decided to share more of my journey and expertise with you. In a more intimate and convenient learning environment for you. How? With the help of The Increase Academy. I have also enlisted the help of my lovely wife, Lady Sandie (after all, she knows me better than anybody else and has been growing and increasing her thinking and mindset alongside me) to go deeper in some key areas that due to space and time constraints I could not explicate on here. I am a storyteller and a teacher, together with my wife, I will teach you what we have learned after many years of marriage, ministry, raising a family, and running several successful businesses.

Inside The digital Increase Academy, you will find practical exercises, video/audio interviews and teachings that will stretch you and increase your thinking. And this is why, I would like to formally and warmly invite you to take a look inside The Increase Academy and take the journey of a lifetime with us. Why? Because you could choose to keep doing the same things that are clearly NOT working, OR, you could choose LIFE. To learn from two people that have also ridden the struggle bus and now get to enjoy the many blessings IN-CREASED thinking affords them. Come learn with us and discover how life can be when you FULLY understand how money works and how to leverage the VERY principles, I shared with you in this book.

Are you ready to learn more and FINAL-LY embrace your God-given identity and position? Then head over to the academy by visiting this link: https://jcm-master-level.teachable.com so you can start your very own Increase Journey. See you inside and, here's to your Increased Thinking.

CHAPTER

CONCLUSION

What is the power of Increased Thinking? I have dreamed of writing and sharing the thoughts and principles inside this book with you for a VERY long time, and once I set my mind to writing them, I was able to finally make this book a reality. Don't think for a second that I am not still learning and being stretched. This journey of increasing one's thinking is not a destination you arrive to and then that's it, not at all. It is the journey of a lifetime (trust me, you wouldn't want it to be any other way). This is a trip I have committed to take until the day I close my eyes on this earth and am taken to heaven.

Every success, triumph or achievement, whether in business, ministry or in my personal life has been attained because of the quality (level) of my thinking. All of them became a reality because I have learned to think how God thinks. Because I have learned to trust I am who God says I am. I know it is easier said than done, but I can tell you this, the rewards are worth EVERY uphill battle you fight with yourself. Yes, most of the time we are our own worse enemies. No wonder one of my favorite quotes is,

"We have met the enemy, and he is us."
Walt Kelly

How does one stop fighting progress, growth, change, and increase? Well, that's a multi-million-dollar question, and I can tell you that it takes putting into practice ALL the principles I shared with you. Making the decision to FINALLY accept that the old ways of thinking NO longer work for you and probably the MOST important one, surrounding yourself with a mentor(s) that speaks your language (has experienced or is familiar with your mindset issues) and is ready, willing and able to guide through the Increase Thinking journey.

It has been a pleasure to spend this 7-chapters with you; I hope you took notes on the margins (that's why I requested they be EXTRA wide for you. You are welcome.) Re-read the parts that challenged you and helped you decide to take the challenge to increase your thinking to the level God has set aside for you before the beginning of your journey here on earth.

God bless you, and may you increase so much others have no choice but to emulate you and join your supernatural growth spur. Feel free to tell someone you love about this book, encourage them to make the investment in their future self and watch how God blesses you and them at the same time.

ABOUT THE AUTHOR

Dr. Chapman is a builder who labors in the vineyard, teaching others how to deepen

spiritually, worship generously and live victoriously! His proclamation style is charismatic and wealthy with practical and transformative truths that help people unlock their inner greatness! The wisdom Dr. Chapman shares helps his listeners make the changes necessary to shift their mindsets and gain lasting success.

An unquenchable passion for helping people is the mark of a man destined for greatness. Dr. Jeffery Chapman is such a man. His heartbeat is to connect every person to God and one another. He serves humanity through his untiring compassion to build others, coupled with his skillful sharing of the timeless truths of God's eternal Word.

As a leading pastor, ministry innovator, entrepreneur and community development

INCREASE: YOU'RE THINKING TOO LOW

strategist, Dr. Jeffery Chapman expends of himself in the expansion of his ministry, the growth of his congregants and the positive development of his community for legacy-level impact.

A consummate servant, Dr. Chapman is the founding and senior pastor of Raleigh North Christian Center, one of the most dynamic congregations in the Triangle area. Growing it from its origins of 9 congregants to its current membership of over 1,600 exemplifies Dr. Chapman's distinguished leadership and unwavering commitment. His devotion to the Word of God and the continuous progression of his ministry was the motivation for his earning a master's degree in Christian Education from Beacon University in Columbus, Georgia and a Doctorate in Theology from North Carolina School of Theology in Wilmington, North Carolina.

Dr. Chapman is a man with an unwavering belief that thriving families are the essential cornerstone for the revitalization of our communities and nation. He has been a devoted husband to his lovely wife and ministry partner, Sandie Monica Chapman for more than 30 years. Together they are blessed to be the parents of three and the grandparents of two.

How to connect with Dr. Chapman:
https://drjefferychapman.org/
https://www.linkedin.com/in/dr-jeffery-chapman-sr/
https://www.instagram.com/drjefferychapman/

Made in the USA
Columbia, SC
18 September 2019